Body Language Analysis

The Most Effective Guide to Speed-Reading People, Body Language Analysis, Psychological Persuasion and Manipulation

SCOTT PRICE

© **Copyright 2020 - All rights reserved.**

This document is geared towards providing exact and reliable information regarding topic and issue covered. The publication is sold with the idea that the publisher is not required to render accounting, officially permitted, or otherwise, qualified services. If advice is necessary, legal or professional, a practiced individual in the profession should be ordered.

- From a Declaration of Principles which was accepted and approved equally by a Committee of the American Bar Association and a Committee of Publishers and Associations.

In no way is it legal to reproduce, duplicate, or transmit any part of this document in either electronic means or in printed format. Recording of this publication is strictly prohibited and any storage of this document is not allowed unless with written permission from the publisher. All rights reserved.

The information provided herein is stated to be truthful and consistent, in that any liability, in terms of inattention or otherwise, by any usage or abuse of any policies, processes, or directions contained within is the solitary and utter responsibility of the recipient reader. Under no circumstances will any legal responsibility or blame be held against the publisher for any reparation, damages, or monetary loss due to the information herein, either directly or indirectly.

Respective authors own all copyrights not held by the publisher.

The information herein is offered for informational purposes solely, and is universal as so. The presentation of the information is without contract or any type of guarantee assurance.

The trademarks that are used are without any consent, and the publication of the trademark is without permission or backing by the trademark owner. All trademarks and brands within this book are for clarifying purposes only and are the owned by the owners themselves, not affiliated with this document.

Table of Contents

How to Analyze People 7

Introduction 8

Chapter 1: Mastering the Art of Analyzing People - Body Language 101 13

Chapter 2: Understanding the Self - What Does My Behavior Display? 21

Chapter 3: It's All in the Eyes - Clues to Revealing True Intentions 27

Chapter 4: The Cues that Tell It All - Context Trumps Words 35

Chapter 5: Essential Tools that Give You an Edge Analyzing Behavior 41

Chapter 6: How to Interpret Verbal Communication 43

Chapter 7: Destroy Perception and Build Understanding 49

Chapter 8: Common Patterns of Interpreting Behavior – Legs and Feet 55

Chapter 9: Common Patterns of Interpreting Behavior - Arms and Hands 61

Chapter 10: How to Spot a Lie - Key Behavior that Indicates Deception 67

Chapter 11: How to Spot Romantic Interest - Body Language Cues that Signal Attraction 75

Chapter 12: How to Spot Insecurity - Small Signs that Show a Lack of Confidence 81

Conclusion 87

Manipulation 89

Introduction 90

Chapter 1: Examining Emotional Manipulation 93

Chapter 2: Tips for Spotting Covert Manipulation Techniques 105

Chapter 3: Why Manipulators Manipulate 115

Chapter 4: Manipulation and Neuro Linguistic Programming 125

Chapter 5: Techniques for Outsmarting Manipulators 135

Chapter 6: Dealing with Manipulation in Relationships 145

Chapter 7: Solid Tips for Increasing Your Self-Esteem 155

Conclusion 160

Persuasion 161

Introduction 162

Section 1 Program Your Mind: Understand Persuasion and How to Use It 165

Chapter 1.1: Traditional Mental Persuasion 169

Chapter 1.2: Putting It into Practice 181

Chapter 1.3: The Six Truths of Persuasion 195

Section 2 Ultimate Influence: How to Use Conversation to Persuade in Any Circumstance 205

Chapter 2.1: Magnetism Is Not Magical: How to Create a Magnetic Personality 209

Chapter 2.2: Steps to Making Casual Conversation 215

Chapter 2.3: It All Starts with 'Hello' 227

Chapter 2.4: How Listening Is a Form of Persuasion 237

Chapter 2.5: What to Do When People Do Not Listen: How to Handle Conflict 247

Conclusion 257

Emotional Intelligence 261

Introduction 262

Chapter 1: History of Emotional Intelligence Models 267

Chapter 2: Solid Tips for Boosting Emotional Self-awareness 287

Chapter 3: Emotional Intelligence and Delaying Gratification 301

Chapter 4: Boost Your Social EQ with These Powerful Verbal and Non-Verbal Clues 313

Chapter 5: Secrets for Developing High Social E.I. 329

Conclusion 345

How to Analyze People

The Complete Psychologist's Guide to Speed Reading People – Analyze and Influence Anyone through Human Behavior Psychology, Analysis of Body Language and Personality Types

Introduction

Congratulations on getting a copy of *How to Analyze People: The Complete Psychologist's Guide to Speed Reading People – Analyze and Influence Anyone through Human Behavior Psychology, Analysis of Body Language and Personality Type.*

Body language can be likened to secret windows of the soul. Since our emotions are intertwined with our behavior, our inner feelings can appear through subtle body movements. Many of these slight changes are so innate, you may not even realize they are happening. Certain emotions like fear, lust, and euphoria can be detected through the manner in which a person moves the body. Many of these expressions are innate and are primal instincts. Much like a baby grasping the finger of his mother, he instinctively is communicating through movement.

One may conclude that understanding body language is a useless skill because we have the gift of verbal communication. While the art of linguistics is certainly necessary to communication, oftentimes, words only tell a small truth. People who lack the proper understanding of the connection between the body and mind will miss these slight signals. For example, the slight curve of the lips combined with a forward lean speaks attraction even if the words being spoken reveal the opposite. Imagine having the ability to detect when someone was lying by observing a simple eye movement.

There is a dynamic structure of the brain called the limbic system that is responsible for controlling how our emotions translate throughout our bodies. The limbic system controls our inner qualities such as the ability to nurture, express empathy, and even react to love. When your face suddenly blushes because you see your crush, that is your brain responding to the emotion of attraction. Without the limbic system, it would be increasingly difficult to be able to openly express our emotions through physical contact.

Animals Use Body Language to Communicate

Dogs are classic examples of animals who rely heavily on body movements to express themselves. Since they cannot verbalize their emotions to humans, they use their ears, paws, and even their tails to signal important symbols. Universally, a dog's tail wagging has been accepted as a dog showing his friendliness. However, not every wag is welcoming. A stiff, low wagging tail can indicate feelings of uneasiness. A straight, pointed wag is a sign of impending attack. Someone who generalizes all tail wagging as welcoming may encounter an unpleasant situation without the proper knowledge. Dog trainers initially begin their training with body movements to assign meanings to commands.

The same mentality rings true with humans. Many people may say one thing to appease the person they are around, yet their true intentions are masked. By understanding the psychology behind body language, you will be able to actually read people without them even knowing it. This ability comes in handy for the following situations:

- Raising a child
- Understanding your mate's true feelings
- Detecting lies or deception
- Spotting insecurity
- Emergency situations

Once mastered, you will be able to further develop your analytical skills and hone in on your ability to decode human behavior.

When raising young children, the ability to effectively communicate needs doesn't become apparent until around 15 months. Babies and toddlers rely heavily on certain nonverbal cues when communicating their needs. For example, children who experience inner conflict and lack the ability to express themselves verbally may bite their parents or peers as a means to seek attention. This oral fixation is their way of getting their needs met. It is important for parents to understand the subtle movements of others in order to accurately meet the needs of their children.

Humans have used body language as a means of communication since the dawn of time. Before the traditional linguistic structure that we see today was developed, our ancestors relied heavily on innate body movements to express true emotions. In 1872, evolutionist Charles Darwin studied the behavior of humans and animals in his book, *The Expression of the Emotions in Man and Animals*. He analyzed carefully how animals communicate non-verbally and made scientific comparisons to humans. Without his groundbreaking revelations, different forms of education like anthropology, social sciences, and even kinesics would be irrelevant. As more psychological evidence has appeared, thus proving the existence of legitimate body cues, we have the ability to assign meanings to intricate expressions.

There are plenty of books on this subject on the market. Thanks again for choosing this one, please enjoy!

Chapter 1: Mastering the Art of Analyzing People - Body Language 101

Body Language Clues: The Basics

When individuals communicate, the face is typically the focal point. The lips are home to revealing contextual clues towards a person's thoughts. For example, when the lips begin to draw inward towards the mouth, a person may be hiding something. They may have a secret or detail they want to share with you, but are apprehensive due to various reasons. This is sometimes known as "lip swallowing" as a person is physically stopping themselves from revealing what they truly want to say.

Many attribute a sad face with the corners of the lips pointing downward. Some individuals rest their lips in this position on a regular basis. This could indicate an inward turmoil or grief they are experiencing. Many of us encounter melancholy individuals whether personally or in the workplace. The next time you are speaking to them, pay attention to the positioning of their lips. You may have a solid backing for viewing them as being generally sad.

People who frequently bite their lips may deal with chronic anxiety or are showing you that they are uncomfortable. Many times, an unpleasant conversation, stress, or nervousness will show through biting. This action is almost like a safe space for individuals as it provides them with comfort in the midst of anxiety.

Signs Given Through the Nose

Although commonly ignored, the nose can signal various emotions such as aggression, displeasure, and even brainstorming. When people are deep in thought, you may notice that they tend to play with the tip of their nose by wiggling or even making an imprint on it. A slight pinch shows frustration; perhaps a person cannot figure out a solution.

You have likely heard the reaction of a person being provoked. However, the nose can signal the true nature of their next move. When the nostrils flare, a person is experiencing a great deal of adrenaline due to feelings of extreme anger. They may be reaching their limit in an argument and gearing themselves up for the next level. When you notice this, perhaps de-escalate the conversation until that person can calm down. They may be using this intense form of breathing as ammunition to explode!

What Your Eyebrows Are Saying

The forehead works in conjunction with the eyes and eyebrows to signal astonishment with slight wonder. Maybe you are retelling an exciting story, and the person doesn't quite believe the extremity of it. Their forehead may wrinkle to indicate disbelief. This doesn't mean they think you are a liar. Rather, they are surprised by the story's context which makes them want to know more.

The eyebrows are just as expressive as the eyes themselves. Since they are flexible to a certain degree, they are able to be animated. As mentioned, a wrinkled forehead can be associated with shock. Often, this is accompanied by raised eyebrows. This positioning of the face is aligned with the common "gasp" expression used in illustrations.

When lowered, the brows can signal a plethora of emotions from confusion to irritation. Speculation is the commonality between the different signals given off by the brows. In addition, a lowered brow could indicate disrespect. In an argument, oftentimes, one misspoken phrase can set off a round of lowered brows followed by the head slanting backwards.

Cartoons may depict a hunky man raising and lowering his eyebrows up and down when looking at an attractive woman. These actions are often expressed in an extreme manner. Although entertaining, illustrators are correct with their depiction. Brows moving in a quick up and down motion can signify recognition. When we run into an old friend at a crowded coffee shop, our eyebrows may quickly jolt up and down.

These are examples of subtle movements taking place in unlikely areas of the face. The eyes were purposely left out as we will dive deeper into their meaning later. Although the face is home to distinct signs of emotion, the body can radiate similar clues to indicate feelings.

Body Cues

When engaging in a conversation, leaning in towards your partner reveals interest. While eating dinner, a woman may lean in towards her date with her entire body pointed in his direction. When this occurs, all areas of the body are facing the subject at hand. Even the fingers, toes, knees, and nose are facing the opposite person. In many instances, legs leaning towards a love interest while sitting could indicate a desire for a sexual encounter.

A hunched back with shoulders pointing inward indicates anxiety or sadness. When the body curls inward, this demonstrates fear. Your body is trying to protect itself instinctively. When a child is embarrassed, you will often notice their head, shoulders, and arms dropping in an obvious manner. In adults, we are conditioned to hide emotions such as embarrassment, anxiety, or fear. Because of this, the signs are subtle. At the root of all emotions such as embarrassment, anxiety, or sadness is fear. Fear of the unknown, fear of what others are thinking, and fear of the future. With the body curling inward, you may suddenly feel safe and less vulnerable. To prove this, imagine a time where you were embarrassed by a mistake at work. Perhaps your boss confronted you about it in a less than ideal manner. Did you have to force your body to stand tall to exude confidence? If so, you probably had to work at holding yourself upright.

The chest is a silent means of flirtation for both men and women. Men may point their chest outward to show masculinity. A woman may entice by pointing her chest towards her interest in order to expose her breasts. In addition, women may slightly turn their chest to about 45 degrees in order to further pronounce their figure.

A chest that is curving inward is a protective mechanism. Animals, as mentioned in the outset, have a similar body language that communicates dominance or submission. When a wolf is showing his alpha that he is not a threat, he will curve his chest inward, thus concealing his strength. This isn't an inviting pose, but rather, a sign that he isn't seeking conflict. Humans display these same tendencies. A successful CEO may relax the chest and position it inward when wanting to appear humble towards employees. This pose, although it translates insecurity, can be a friendly, submissive gesture, perhaps even signaling respect.

Signs of the Shoulders, Neck, and Hips

In a similar fashion, when the shoulders, neck, and back are upright, this person is demonstrating confidence. However, the need for authoritative power could shift the shoulders from an upright positioning to one that looms over as a means to show intimidation. Notice how the shoulders, even though being portrayed as upright, still slightly curl. Although this person is clearly trying to establish authority, there is still a slight insecurity or protection in his stance. This is a key sign in revealing people who may appear confident, but are truly insecure about something deep down.

The back is powerful and direct. When you are conversing with someone, and they keep their back turned away from you, likely, they are not interested in what you have to say. In addition, this could be another sign of attempting to give off dominance. This dismissive behavior is condescending to the person they are engaging with and makes them less approachable.

The hips make subtle movements but powerful demands. Generally, the hips are used with sexual communication, thus inviting or rejecting a potential partner. When pushed outward or swayed, the invitation for flirtation is abundant. A person may show their attraction in this manner. Similarly, the direction that the hips are pointing towards could also signal the direction that person wants to go.

Body language is a beautiful tool that allows truth to emanate. Body language is all about association.

The directions that we typically link to emotions can reveal the true state of a person. In order to effectively master this language, it's important to understand basic psychological principles. When assigning deeper meaning to common motion, you are thinking like a psychologist. As mentioned, the previous examples only scratch the surface to what the body is telling us. As we dive into the complexities of body language, you will see how intricate and detailed this communication form truly is.

Chapter 2: Understanding the Self - What Does My Behavior Display?

In order to properly analyze others, it is important to seek understanding with your own body movements. In social settings, the way we position our body can be the difference between making friends and repelling them. Since we cannot see our body movements as well as others, it's important to become in tune with your feelings and perception. Many times, we may not even realize the silent signals we are giving off. Sure, we have the ability to speak our emotions, but we all know that the truth is seldom spoken.

Science has proven that we emit energy that can be detected, and is even contagious. When your inner energy is feeling tired or bored, your outward appearance will give evidence of that energy despite how "excited" you say you are. Technology has given us the grand opportunity to display rejection with the simple glance down at the phone. For example, when a friend is telling you a story that you are 100 percent not interested in, likely you will reach for your phone and begin scrolling. Your words are saying, "Uh-huh," occasionally, but your demeanor speaks volumes. You may believe you are listening when really you are showing outward disdain for your friend. This sign is often taken as disrespect and could create distance in the friendship.

Another common sign is the crossing of the arms. In social occasions, this can be translated as, "I don't want to be here." When in reality, you could simply be cold. Since this is what you are exhibiting, others are naturally going to view you as unapproachable. Do you find yourself doing this quite often? Crossing of the arms is another form of protection. It is almost likened to a comfort mechanism that we do when in an uncomfortable situation.

This can be attributed to a form of social anxiety and inner insecurity. Sure, you may be the most inviting person in the room, but you are not aware of that yet. Your inner, primal voice is activating your fight or flight response. You may be subconsciously uncomfortable with your outfit, afraid of others' opinions, or even fearful of talking to people. The importance of becoming aware of your deeper desires will work wonders towards your body language.

Another instance occurs during one-on-one communication. Do you notice your eyes drifting during a conversation? Or even your hand being placed on your face while someone is talking? This signals disinterest and could be extremely disrespectful to the person talking. In turn, your friend could become upset with you without you even realizing it.

Flirtation can be a fine and tricky art because many of the signals of genuine interest and attraction are often intertwined. For example, a young man was engaging in a conversation with a married woman at a public event. She was talking to him about a job opportunity she had available in her department. Being recently laid off from his job, naturally, the man was excited! He began to shift his body towards her as he leaned his head in. His eyes never left hers, and he had a slight smile on his face. Upon noticing, the woman's husband grew increasingly alert to their conversation. From the outside, all he saw was this young man, leaning in towards his wife with a smile. Unbeknownst to him, the situation was far from flirtatious.

This is a clear indicator of how our body language deeply affects the way people view us. When engaging in that conversation, the young man was extremely interested in the possible job opportunity, not the married woman. However, his body language signaled attraction. The importance of being aware of how your body is positioned when speaking to others is a subliminal sign of respect. One fantastic way to become aware of your body motions is to remember the three W's: who, what, and where. Let's consider them one at a time.

Who

When speaking with another person, it's key to remember who you are engaging with. Is it a close friend of the opposite sex? Is it your manager or maybe even an older person? In all of these instances, the way you position your body means everything. Take, for example, speaking with your manager. Do you find yourself naturally crossing your arms when he or she approaches you? This could be your way of protecting yourself against their authority, or you may actually dislike your manager. However, you want to keep your job and even appear interested in what he or she has to say. This instance is when acting and awareness play a major role.

When you see your manager coming, the butterflies may ensue. You may even become a bit clammy in the hands. Instead of allowing that feeling to overpower you, simply acknowledge it, and let it be. Don't try to manipulate the feeling as that causes further anxiety. Rather, acknowledge it, and place your hands by your side with open palms. Try your best to breathe and remain comfortable. Position your back upright with your shoulders aligned. Create an opening demeanor that opens the door for conversation.

What

When engaging in a conversation, try to feel what your body is doing. Are your hands clenched in a fist? Do you feel your face tightening as if you're displeased? When you become aware of what your body does when engaging in a conversation, you will be able to control those muscles. One vital question you can ask yourself is, "What is my body telling others right now?" By doing so, you can immediately change the way others perceive you.

Where

It's especially important to be cognizant of where you are when speaking to others. Oftentimes, certain atmospheres may warrant specific behavior. For example, during a blind date, it would be quite rude to scrunch your forehead and brows in disgust at your date's appearance. Sure, they may not be what you expected, but you never want to display your inner emotions. In addition, you wouldn't walk into a funeral with a big smile and open arms. Even if you barely knew the deceased, that demeanor may appear heartless to the grieving family. Making the connection between what your body is doing and remembering where you are is imperative for your reputation.

Body awareness is key to navigating your world. It is defined as "the sense that we have of our own bodies." It is an understanding of the parts that make up one's body, where they are located, how they feel, and even what they can do. Certain activities such as yoga and Pilates assist with connecting the bridge between the body and mind. When engaging in these exercises, you are mentally aware of the positioning of your body. You have full control over your balance which strengthens your mental and physical muscles. Engaging in these activities on a regular basis can assist with understanding your body movements. This will come in handy when evaluating what your body is doing in social settings.

To practice your own proprioception exercise at home, begin by balancing on one foot. What are your arms doing? Your fingers? Do you feel a tingle in your opposing leg? Become engrossed in how your body is working together to keep you balanced. By repeating this simple exercise daily, you'll begin to notice the movements of even the smallest parts of your body.

In order to fully understand the body language of others, you have to become connected with your personal movements. Body language is more than just reading movements. It's attributing a deeper meaning towards body posture that can speak volumes into a person's emotions.

Chapter 3: It's All in the Eyes - Clues to Revealing True Intentions

When children are being evaluated for neurological challenges, one of the main observable points is their ability to maintain good eye contact. Although an intricate detail, the ability to lock eyes with someone else during conversation speaks wonders to the child's level of function. If a child is able to maintain direct eye contact throughout the course of their assessments, they are deemed high on the social spectrum. However, the inability to maintain eye contact could be a sign of autism or even social anxiety. The eyes reveal small truths to the inner workings of our biology.

Typically, what is the first thing you look at when meeting someone? Usually, their eyes reveal aspects of beauty that are attractive to first encounters. Many even remember people because of the shape, color, and size of the eyes. We are neurotically programmed to be visual creatures who make associations through what we see. Generally, these associations are labeled by what we give off. Since every aspect of the body works in conjunction with the brain, how do our eyes communicate with certain receptors?

The Eye Meets the Brain

The retina is like the gatekeeper of the eye. Everything we see, through the exchange of light, passes through the retina and is then transferred to two different aspects of the eye: rods which manage our ability to see at night, and cones which handle our daily vision activities such as color translation, reading, writing, and scanning. Various neurons travel throughout the eye and communicate with different functions within the eye to carry unique signals. These signals are then carried through the optic nerve into the cerebral cortex. The cerebral cortex is like the movie theatre of the brain. It controls our visual receptors that are responsible for perception, memory, and thoughts. When our eye sees something pleasurable, researchers have discovered that the pupil actually expands. This phenomenon proves that what we see is how we think. Through this, we can formulate opinions, draw conclusions, and even interpret body movements.

There are certain concrete directions carried out by the eyes that indicate true intentions:

Right glance: This is used to remember something, maybe a name, face, song, or book.

Left glance: This is used to remember physical features such as color, shape, texture, and other visual stimulants.

Glancing downward in a right position: This controls our imagination and what we believe something to be like.

Glancing downward towards the left: Inner communication, the conversations we have with the self.

The way our eyes work with the brain and perception is key to understanding body language. Since we use every aspect of our body to communicate, it is only natural that the eyes play a major role in this form of communication. Sure, the eyes may seem one dimensional to the untrained individual. However, their slight movements can indicate everything you need to know about a person. Let's consider a few examples.

Direct Eye Contact

Direct eye contact can mean a caveat of emotions. Surely, self-confidence is one of the primary indicators of locking eyes. When vetting for a job, recruiters will often instruct their interviewees to look the interviewer in the eye in order to display awareness. This shows the interviewer that you aren't intimidated and can take on any task. Similarly, animals utilize eye contact when interpreting dominance. For example, a trainer will often look a dog in the eye that he is training in order to establish dominance. By the trainer locking eyes and refusing to move, the dog will know to listen to his commands. Humans also communicate via dominant signals. Direct eye contact trumps fear. It shows that you are comfortable with the conversation, and it even indicates interest.

In addition, balance is the key to everything. Too much direct eye contact could prove to be intimidating to the receiving individual. This intense stare could cause others to feel uncomfortable, with them maybe even questioning your overall sanity. Imagine engaging in a conversation with someone who never stopped looking into your eyes. Even when you looked away, their eyes were still locked on yours. Surely, you would chalk them up to be extremely strange. It's always important to be cognizant of what your eyes are doing as staring, in some cultures, could be viewed as rude.

Looking Away

When a person avoids eye contact, this is typically a sign of low self-confidence. The person may be uncomfortable with the conversation, person, or environment they are in. In addition, anxiety surrounding social settings can make a person apprehensive to locking eyes with someone they don't know. Avoiding eye contact also signals inner conflict. Perhaps they are fighting against subconscious urges of attraction; therefore, they avoid making eye contact; or maybe they are hiding something that heightens their anxiety. This doesn't indicate that a person is devious or even untrustworthy. They may suffer from debilitating self-consciousness that overwhelms their disposition.

Dilated Pupils

The pupils generate intricate signals that identify even the smallest of changes within the body. Studies have shown that when people are presented with a challenging question, their pupils grow larger. When the brain is forced to think beyond its capabilities, the pupils actually become narrow, according to a 1973 study. The pupils are also key indicators of stress on the brain. Health care professionals will shine a small flashlight into the eyes of their patients in order to check the normality of their pupils. If the pupils are balanced in size and react to the shining light, the brain isn't experiencing distress. However, any imbalance could indicate a serious brain injury.

As mentioned earlier, dilated pupils express extreme interest, even agreement. When you see or hear something that sparks your attention, your pupils will dilate almost immediately. The same occurs when a person is shown a representation of something they agree with. In 1969, a revered researcher sought to prove the notion that the pupils' dilation can reveal political affiliations. By showing participants pictures of political figures they admired, the participants' eyes dilated.

However, when shown an opposing photo, the pupils grew narrow; often snake-like.

What Our Visual Directions Indicate

The positioning of our eyes and what we choose to focus on during a conversation can speak volumes. For instance, glancing downward could indicate shame, even submission. When children are being reprimanded, they are often looking down to show their personal disdain for their behavior. In ancient Chinese culture, one typically looked down in a submissive form to show respect to those in authority. On the contrary, glaring upward indicated traits of haughtiness. It is often associated with being bored or not wanting to engage in the activity at hand. In addition, looking up signals uncertainty. Movies and television shows may depict a teenager taking a test and looking up because they are unaware of the answer.

Sideways glances are often cues for internal irritation. For example, when a co-worker you dislike walks into the room, you may inadvertently look at them sideways, simply because they are the bane of your existence. This can also occur when engaging with individuals who annoy you. The takeaway from the sideways stare is discontentment. When you see something that just isn't right, or even a sneaky individual, you may give them the side-eye. This demonstrates total repulsion for their attitude, reputation, or even their expressions.

Many would attribute squinting to being unable to see. While true, a squint can also mimic signs of disbelief or confusion. One may hear something and want more information. Thus, they squint their eyes while listening; it's almost as if they are saying, "I don't believe you…I need more answers!"

Stress can induce quick blinking which causes a person to go into a frenzy. You may notice a person rapidly blinking while moving frantically to finish a task. This could be accompanied by sweat or trembling. On the contrary, excessive blinking could be a subtle sign of arrogance. A boss, for example, may blink rapidly while speaking to an employee in an attempt to dismiss their conversation. This fast-action blinking essentially blinds the boss from the employee for less than a second, indicating that they would rather be engaging in something else.

A direct gaze paired with a lowered lid and head indicates extreme attraction. It's almost likened to a "come hither" invitation between mates. This gaze is heightened through sexual attraction and may even induce pupil dilation.

Inability to Focus and Attention Deficit

An eye nystagmus identifies how long it takes the body to focus on one point after undergoing extreme movement. If a person has a nystagmus lasting longer than 14 seconds, they may have challenges with keeping focused. One academic facility tests the accuracy of a child's nystagmus by spinning them a number of times and having them glance up towards the ceiling. The eyes then move rapidly, sometimes dilating, then narrowing. The longer it takes the child to stabilize is documented. They further engage in this spinning activity weekly with the hopes of strengthening their ability to remain focused on one thing despite many distractions. As they continue to grow a tolerance, their eyes will stabilize in a lower amount of time. The goal is to strengthen their ability to dismiss outward distractions which will help with attention deficit disorder. The movement of the eyes tell trained professionals exactly how much assistance a child will need and in what specific area. Aren't the eyes magnificent?

Our eyes open the door to many revelations of the self. You are able to gain psychological perspective on how you perceive yourself and others by a simple glance! Irritation, lust, attraction, and even doubt can be detected by paying close attention. Since the eyes have a direct pathway to the brain, it is only natural that they are the gatekeepers of the soul. By implementing these quick tips into your social life, you will have the grand ability to analyze a person in a complex manner. Of course, the eyes are also home to detecting deceit. As we continue to travel through our body language adventure, we will soon learn how the eyes can reveal the trustworthiness of an individual.

Chapter 4: The Cues that Tell It All - Context Trumps Words

Universally, there are certain facial expressions that demolish all cultural divides. Researchers conclude that all over the world, happiness, sadness, surprise, fear, disgust, and anger are all expressed in the same manner. Gesturing, as well as touching, gives off certain signals that assist with emotions.

However, nonverbal communication essentially means reading between the lines and seeking truth in the midst of words. A person may be saying one thing, but their tone means another. Researchers have grouped nonverbal communication into five categories. Let's consider them each.

1. Repetition

When engaging in a conversation, it is useful to repeat what the other person has said so as to improve memory. When a person verbally repeats what you said to them, they are demonstrating that your statement matters. They want to be able to access that information at a later time. In addition, this may be used as a signal that they are listening to what you're saying. Be careful, though, as too much repetition could be an irritation to some. They may misunderstand your listening cues as condescending as this is what mothers do to children when they learn to speak.

2. Contradiction

Contradiction is one of the more obvious cues that signal disapproval. Often times, these subtle contradictions could be used to demean another or express dominance. One of the primary examples of this occurs in the workplace. For example, a controlling manager overhears her employee speaking with a customer. The customer is asking about a specific protocol. The employee is attempting to describe an easier way to accomplish her goal. Upon hearing, the manager immediately steps in, tells the employee that her way is incorrect and proceeds to direct the customer herself. Imagine how that employee feels. Not only was she embarrassed in front of a client, but her notability was questioned. This contradiction caused the customer to view the employee as someone who isn't well-versed. The manager could have handled the situation in a more graceful manner, and likely, this was done out of an attempt to prove dominance.

3. Substitutions

Do you remember that look your mother gave you when she meant what she said? Likely, you can envision those stern eyes, scrunched mouth, and serious demeanor. Your mother didn't have to utter one phrase for you to understand that your current behavior was unacceptable. Daily, we use substitutions as a means to communicate. These intense glares or slight glances can speak volumes to people who know each other well. They may also indicate emphasis on a certain command. Dogs operate primarily through vocal substitutions. When you loom over a dog while stating, "Back," they know that area is off limits to them. The actual word is being substituted for an understandable action.

4. Complimenting

When a young man performs well at his baseball game, onlookers can see the coach patting him on the back or even giving him a high five. These outward displays of approval are well-known cues that signify a job well done. We may give a wink, hand gesture, or even a hug to express proud emotions towards others. This mild stamp of approval crosses masculine and feminine roles as well. Football players are often seen patting the butts of their teammates to signify a job well done. When conducted between romantic interests, this could be an outward sexual invitation.

5. Accenting

This occurs when people want their voices to be heard. They may slam their bedroom doors after yelling a remark, or clap their hands to express seriousness. This can be likened to accenting a specific word. That small dash brings emphasis to one or more of the noted letters. Thus, it alerts the reader to change their pronunciation. Similarly, accenting in nonverbal cues could signal a change of behavior. When analyzing individuals with deep-rooted insecurities, they may rely heavily on accenting their words in order to appear dominant. They are hoping to ignite fear in their subjects as a means of control.

Gestures can accentuate a conversation and create excitement. Typically, individuals who utilize gestures are described as, "people who talk with their hands." These movements can emphasize the plot of a story or even bring light to a discourse. They are descriptive in nature, and are used to keeping the attention of an audience or an individual. Public speaking classes place a great deal of weight on the importance of using gestures in their delivery. They bring warmth to the words being spoken in addition to liveliness.

One of the primary ways to build a human connection is through touch. The embracing touch coming from a friend or a stranger can alleviate stress and create a sense of community. When grieving, oftentimes, words from well-intended individuals are not enough. However, a soft touch of the hand speaks, "I am here for you," in a way that words could never express. The reason being is that touching is an action. You are physically showing someone your interest in them. In addition, touching hands can signify a person's personality. Certain managers judge potential candidates based upon their handshake. If they encounter a weak shake, the boss can pick up on their timid nature. They may shy away from hiring them in a fast-paced environment. On the other hand, a firm shake exudes confidence. The hiring manager may consider that candidate because they didn't display fear.

Across various cultures, the amount of personal space given is varied. East Asian cultures typically stand about one to two inches away from the person they are engaging with. This displays a sign of respect and interest. In the United States, however, we may view that spatial closeness as intruding. We may even feel uncomfortable as to what the person's intentions are. However, creating too much space could trigger your householder into thinking you don't want to be around them. Creating a balanced view of spatial awareness is important to communicating effectively. Take a look at the distance between the tip of your pointer finger and your inner elbow.

This is the proper amount of allotted space that will allow you to converse comfortably with your partner.

The manner in which someone speaks can also indicate personality traits. Usually, grade school teachers will speak to their students in a high-pitched voice, as it ignites excitement and is inviting. However, that level of excitement may not be warranted at an all-adult function. In fact, if they tried to speak to another adult in that manner, the receiving adult may take it as the person being condescending. It is useful to consider the tone in which you are speaking so as not to come off as being rude, sarcastic, or even flirty. Creating a balanced manner of speaking while interjecting inflections when necessary will help you to effectively communicate without offense.

Nonverbal communication can be acquired through analyzing simple cues that occur daily. You may ask yourself, "When someone speaks to me in this way, how do I feel?" or, "Am I comfortable when someone else is this close to me?" By asking yourself these simple questions, you will be able to effectively communicate with others while picking up on their cues.

Chapter 5: Essential Tools that Give You an Edge Analyzing Behavior

The next section will get into the "bread and butter" of our discussion. Body language is an entire psychology that assigns significant reasons behind behavior. Understanding these reasons will give you dominance over others because it emphasizes humanity. You are taking the additional time to become educated on understanding someone else. This places great emphasis on empathy as it forces you to become connected with another human. Imagine being able to understand the context of what someone else is saying as opposed to taking their words literally. You will likely be able to communicate effectively and make strategic moves. You will no longer obsess over small intricacies as you will already have the definitive answer. As you read, imagine someone in your life who displays the qualities presented. How have you previously engaged with them? Has your experience been positive or negative? Have your misunderstandings sparked the need to resolve conflict or ignite it? When you learn how to "work the system," so to speak, you will gain insight into how to effectively break the barriers of communication and emphasize understanding. These tools are imperative to your reputation, social success, and even productivity. When seeking to gain a better understanding of the behavior of others, it's wise to consider these three aspects:

1. Can I separate my previous preconceived notions from what is occurring in front of me?
2. Can I somehow make a valuable difference in this person's life by picking up on their social cues?
3. Am I willing to confront situations of deceit or attraction head on so as to fulfill my personal needs?
4. The ability to read the language of others comes with a weighty responsibility. You are essentially able to decode truth. You must then develop a proper way to confront certain revelations head on. This is where building your ability to effectively communicate comes into play. By learning how to state your opinion without embarrassing the other person, you can use your new talent for the betterment of society.

Chapter 6: How to Interpret Verbal Communication

A young student has worked over 20 hours to complete a 40-page essay for her college class. She then had to develop a visual representation to accompany her presentation. After three restless nights and countless cups of coffee, she is finally ready to present her finished report to the class. After performing an engaging and educational discourse, she breathed a deep sigh of relief. After class, she approached her professor and asked him how he enjoyed it. Barely looking up from his computer, the professor stopped and said, "It was fine," in a monotone voice. She was devastated. After dedicating all of her time and resources to this project, she was not satisfied with, "It was fine." A week later, after wondering what she could have improved upon, she finally got her grade back. Shaking, she opened the link and saw a 100% grade. She was ecstatic. She felt greatly accomplished and proud of her work. However, she still wondered why the professor gave her that response if he was going to give her an A.

The professor could have genuinely loved her presentation. In fact, it could have given him chills. However, because he was so monotone in his response, the student grew insecure. He gave off the impression that he did not appreciate all of her hard work. In reality, the professor greatly enjoyed it; so much so, he gave her a perfect grade. What is the issue with his actions?

Likely, you would conclude that the way he uttered, "It was fine," was a turn off. That monotone delivery is quite different from the excited, "It was fine!" paired with a clap. This is the power of verbal communication. Although one person may say one thing, the way they speak it reveals the truth. Our body language works closely with the manner in which we speak. A rather rude comment can be overlooked when paired with a smiling face, or it could be taken as extremely creepy. In addition, a smile can hide insidious intentions. This is why body language is a compilation of various components.

When a person constantly speaks in a harsh, assertive, and bold manner, others may conclude that that person is angry. They may even avoid associating with them for fear of embracing negative energy. In reality, the person could be amicable and positive. However, the way they place great emphasis on certain words or topics is intimidating. The power of tone, emphasis, and volume can create great conclusions when it comes to reputation. However, there are exceptions to this theory. Some individuals may express themselves one way, yet their actual personality is quite different. Take, for example, the late Michael Jackson. Michael had an extremely light and timid voice. He would speak almost like an unsure child, retelling a bedtime story. Upon only hearing him, one may conclude that Michael was submissive, shy, and quiet. The reality of his persona was quite different. The innovation found within his music and the creativity exuded through his dance moves illuminated great power and confidence. Despite the volume, tone, and inflection of his voice, he was a mighty lion when it came to his craft. Personal friends and family members, however, knew that somewhere, deep inside, lived a submissive, shy, and quiet person. This denotes that within our voice, despite intention, lie deep-rooted personality traits that we may be blind to. The loud and boisterous individual may be seeking to compensate for a deep insecurity. The arrogant and assertive lawyer may be fuming with angry emotions. The way in which a person speaks is complex and reveals truth.

The power behind how you say something can turn your innovative idea into a passed opportunity. Imagine pitching an idea for a new innovation with a monotone voice and no sign of excitement. Surely, those on the other end would not be convinced this is your passion. You may have missed your opportunity simple because you lacked enthusiasm. Your voice can also be a manipulative tool used to assert to others. There is a stark distinction between yelling rules and explaining them. The way a person says something can make a difference in how the sentence is perceived. A stressed manager can assert, "Why are you always late?" to an employee with a stern voice and a frowning mouth. Or she could kindly say, "Why are you always late?" with a slight touch on the shoulder and a concerned tone. This could be the moment where the employee either opens up or seeks further employment. When you think about it, words are just extensions of the mind. We all use them and express ourselves in one way or the other. However, the tone can drastically alter our perceived intentions and even our reputation.

The volume in which one speaks can ignite action. A whisper may indicate confidential information, while a loud yelp could signal, "Get away." In addition, a monotone voice could indicate disinterest where an emphasis on words and syllables could signal excitement. Sarcasm, on the other hand, is quite tricky to decode as it is subjective to the person speaking. One lively individual could show sarcasm in the same manner they would offer a greeting. This is where contextual clues come into play. Analyze the person's body language. Do they have a slight smile or a straight face? Does what they say seem outlandish in relation to the topic at hand? Interpreting sarcasm involves integrative techniques to understanding. It is a complex system that is unique to each person. One of the primary reasons why sarcasm is so difficult to understand for some is because it can mimic traditional body language cues. In this respect, it may be essential to get to know the person you are speaking with, so they can better understand your personality. Then, little by little, bring on the sarcasm!

Understanding your personal inflection can affect your reputation. You may have the purest of intentions, but your diction, volume, and choice of words is taken adversely. Others may create a distance between themselves and you due to this inconsistency. Being cognizant of the way you say something can be a true indicator of your intention. In addition, your communication skills will operate smoothly. The two main components of mastering effective communication are control and awareness. It is important to control the tone, inflection, and volume of your voice. It may even be necessary to control the type of words you use. Next, being aware of your audience, surroundings, and mood can play a huge role in how your words come off. A bad or melancholy mood may not be suitable for a children's book reading at the library. You can practice altering your verbal skills by seeking feedback from others. Have them analyze how you express a sentence, and they can provide constructive ways to improve.

Chapter 7: Destroy Perception and Build Understanding

Unfortunately, many missed opportunities, acts of violence, and lapses of judgment occur due to inaccurate perception. Many people lose the opportunity to connect with others because they rely so heavily on initial judgment. Perception is defined as, "the ability to see, hear, or become aware of something through the senses." We gather conclusions about people from the information we receive from them. If we have a negative encounter, likely, we will perceive that person in a bad light. Body language and perception are the two components that equal a conclusion. The way someone positions themselves, holds their hands, or even moves their eyes can be taken a certain way. Although perceiving body language is a natural part of social development, perception can always be altered. We have the grand ability to be able to acknowledge something without jumping to conclusions. Is this really possible when interpreting body language?

Absolutely! One of the primary keys to building understanding is letting go of preconceived associations. For example, a young woman is always standing with her hands crossed, eyes lowered, and mouth downturned. Upon looking at her, you could conclude that she is prudish, stuck up, and distant. This may prevent you from speaking to her. In reality, the young woman is far from stuck up. Rather, she suffers from social anxiety and is uncomfortable in large crowds. She has a fear of carrying on a conversation along with personal insecurities. She desperately wants to make friends but doesn't want to make the first move. This disconnect creates a whirlwind of false notions that prevents pure human connection. Since one person perceives her as being stuck up, they avoid sparking a conversation without truly getting to know her personality. This occurs often and is the result of misunderstandings.

Breaking down those preconceived notions about certain behavior involves eliminating one-way thinking. As opposed to assigning only one meaning to a specific body movement, open your mind to the possibility of other reasonings behind behavior. Environmental factors may even alter traditional body language meanings. Crossed arms usually translate to feelings of self-consciousness or disapproval. However, in an extremely cold room, does it have the same meaning? When talking with a friend during a sunny day, does their looking to the side mean they are lying? Or could the sun be extraordinarily bright? Situational factors are also imperative to drawing definite conclusions. Breaking eye contact doesn't automatically mean your friend isn't interested in your conversation. Perhaps they are fatigued or swamped with personal issues at the moment. It's important to be flexible with how you perceive behavior. By understanding that there is always a reason behind everything, you will learn to give others the benefit of the doubt.

The traditional saying, "You can't judge a book by its cover," is vital to making social connections. A woman with scrunched brows, a downturned mouth, and hooded eyes may give off the impression that she is always angry. However, upon getting to know her, you realize she is extremely friendly. Perhaps that is the natural structure of her face. The same rings true for a man who engages in deep eye contact, leans in towards his subjects, and touches hands as he speaks. These clues may indicate that he is romantically interested in whomever he is talking to. In reality, that may be his way of showing interest in the conversation. It could almost be likened to respect.

Cultural differences may influence how we perceive certain behavior. For example, in the United States, we typically nod our head signifying, "Yes." However, in Greek cultures, a head nod means "No." In Portugal, individuals may tug their ears when something tastes delicious. Comical, yet true, Italians interpret this as a suggestive move with sexual undertones. Europeans kiss openly in public, whereas traditional Asian countries view this as inappropriate in public. The man mentioned earlier whose mannerisms may be suggestive probably grew up predominantly around women. His mother, no doubt, taught him how to show respect and interest to those to whom he is speaking. Although his actions came off as flirtatious, he was simply acting on a natural impulse. When analyzing others, it's key to remember that everyone comes from a different family that implemented different expectations for behavior. Some families may communicate through touching and warm embraces while another maintains a respectful distance. Before taking offense, consider how they grew up in conjunction with their personality. Perhaps they truly like you, and they are showing you in their own unique way.

Another key way to destroy perception from initial judgment is to get to know the person. Sure, someone may come off as rude, shy, aloof, or even angry. However, are they less deserving of having a social connection with you? Have they done anything concrete that prevents you from associating with them? The initial breaking of the ice may be challenging, but the results are worth it. When approaching someone who gives off negative body language, it's important to consider these tips if attempting to make a connection:

- Ask them about their interests.
- Discuss commonalities and attempt to make a connection.
- Ask them about their family. Do they have siblings? Is their family near or far?
- Share something special about yourself. This may open the door for further conversation.
- Simply ask them how their day is going.

There are a plethora of ice breakers that can be used to approach someone who may seem unapproachable. By doing so, you will learn that, although perception is key, understanding is what shapes relationships. You could be passing up on a purposeful friendship because of a misunderstanding. By taking the additional time to understand someone else, you will then understand their body language. You will learn what encompasses their inner being. This will help you to develop an open mind when building relationships.

Chapter 8: Common Patterns of Interpreting Behavior – Legs and Feet

When engaging in a conversation, we typically don't pay attention to the movements of the lower body. Since our direct line of sight is from the chest up, we often miss the obvious signs of the legs and feet. Certain stances that occur within the legs can signify dominance, sexual attraction, and even anxiety. Let's consider a few common patterns to look for when attempting to analyze someone else.

Crossed Legs

Crossed legs could indicate defensiveness. Perhaps you are sitting in a meeting at work, and your colleague says something totally off-putting. You may find yourself slowly crossing your legs as a subliminal way of showing your disapproval. Defensiveness could be heightened when one hand is positioned on top of the crossed leg. This is almost like a taunting move, signaling combat.

Crossing the ankles or knees are signs of nervousness, anxiety, and fear. This stance is protective in nature, which indicates that someone is attempting to protect themselves from whatever source of fear they are encountering. It could also be a means to control actions during high adrenaline situations.

Pointing and Active Legs

If you are miserable at a party, likely your legs are pointed towards the door as you are ready to leave. Our legs inadvertently point to where our heart wants to go. This can be used to determine interest and attraction. The legs, even when covered, will almost always point in the direction they are interested in.

Legs that bounce continuously could mean two things: boredom and nervousness. When you witness a person continuously bouncing their legs up and down, they may be nervous about something. This bounce is like a protective blanket that distracts their mind from their jitters. In addition, when someone is growing restless and ready to go, they may move their legs rapidly. The bouncing or tapping of the legs can be likened to a compulsion carried out to make the irritation subside.

When both legs point in one direction, it could be a clear indicator of interest for the person. However, when one leg steps back, it could indicate that the person wants distance. They may be uncomfortable with the person, conversation, or situation at hand. This subtle movement could be their way of escaping something distressful.

Messages from the Thighs

The upper portions of the legs usually indicate sexual or suggestive invitations between men and women. In daily activities, men may sit with their thighs opened as a sign of dominance. This outward display of masculinity represents an "alpha male" mentality. With women, closed thighs are a polite sign of femininity. Many young girls are instructed to sit with their legs closed so as not to expose their private areas. This closed manner of sitting is graceful and emanates class. When opened, they express dominance and even a form of female rebellion. Since it is so common for girls to be taught to keep their legs closed, doing the opposite could indicate opposition to societal norms. In addition, it is also extremely flirtatious to sit with the thighs crossed and one sitting higher above the other. This could indicate interest.

The Feet

The feet work very closely with the legs to determine areas of interest. When the toes are pointed at a specific object or direction, this indicates where we want to go. This could be a subtle signal your body sends to your mind about certain situations. The feet are used to make a statement and could also be used as an accent to verbal cues. Stomping, imaginative kicking, or tapping are all means of gaining attention.

When toddlers throw tantrums, it's not only their flailing arms, crying eyes, and yelling demands that occur. Toddlers utilize their legs and feet to create loud noises to further emphasize their anger.

Much like moving the legs, bouncing the feet or excessive pacing are signs of anxiety. During moments of high adrenaline, the feet can be seen moving uncontrollably, almost like rabbit's feet. Signs of nervousness are also present when the feet are curled behind an object, perhaps the legs of a chair or a table. Since curving the body inward is a subtle sign of inner protection, the feet follow suit with this protective stance.

Professor Geoffrey Beattie of the University of Manchester reveals that subtle foot movements and positioning could reveal signs of personality traits. He explains, "The weird thing about feet is that most people know what they are doing with their facial expressions; they may or may not know what they are doing with their hands, but unless we specifically think about it, we know nothing about what we are doing with our feet." Through his studies, he found that individuals with rather arrogant or haughty personalities typically kept their feet still as they were always aware of the self; whereas, shy individuals frequently shuffled their feet when sitting. This gives us insight into the characteristics of a person. Typically, shy people indicate high levels of nervousness or anxiety during social occasions. This directly proves the notion that foot movement equals anxiety. The beauty behind interpreting subtle body movements is that you can always find a glimmer of proof to solidify the theory.

Feet are also directly related to laughter. When we are extremely tickled by something, our feet come slightly off the ground. We may even partner that laughter with a slap of the knee. Dr. Beattie mentioned that men and women subconsciously show their attraction by combining feet movement during laughter. This indicates that the woman is comfortable enough with you to make obvious movements. As far as men, he says, "With men, feet aren't so important. With men it's more head tilting. Women often tilt their heads, and it is often thought to be a feminine thing. But actually, it's men who play a slightly more submissive role."

When it comes to interpreting the signs of the legs and feet, direction and movement are the two primary components needed for translation.

Although we typically fret from glancing at the bottom half of a person, simple movements could be a key indicator as to how a person is feeling. It's imperative to understand the beauty of intricate movements in order to fully understand the inner workings of another person.

Chapter 9: Common Patterns of Interpreting Behavior - Arms and Hands

A great deal of our emotions are expressed through our arms and hands. The warm embrace of a touch indicates love while a sharp slap translates to anger. Much of our productivity depends on the accuracy of our arms and hands when completing tasks. The movements of the arms and hands are quite obvious as they are used as a complement to verbal expression. Let's consider a few subliminal signals we receive from analyzing the hands and arms.

As our arms expand, we typically appear larger than our normal demeanor. This could be used as a descriptive means to explain how massive a person or object is, or this could be a subtle sign of instigating aggression or dominance. It also indicates spatial awareness. A person could expand the arms to give the subtle signal that they prefer space. It could be likened to "marking their territory." On the contrary, when the arms expand but curve towards the person, this is reminiscent of a hug. This embrace indicates safety or protection. Many mother figures are seen welcoming their children in this manner.

Since we primarily use our hands and arms to gesture, they are extremely descriptive tools that express our emotions. When the arms are raised, this is a sign of frustration and overwhelming doubt. We can almost envision an overwhelmed person clenching their hands over their ears or on top of the head as a means of protection.

The crossing of the arms is a true indicator of how a person is feeling. As previously mentioned, when the arms are crossed, this typically means anxiety, shyness, fear, or disbelief. We can picture a frustrated mother or father crossing their arms towards their child when they do something naughty. However, when the arms are tightly crossed with the hands either balled into fists or nestled in the armpits, this signals combat. This occurs when an individual has been taunted. Their anger is essentially holding their arms inward as a protective means. The hidden fists could signal the person holding themselves back from doing something they would regret.

Individuals who have been exposed to violence or who feel vulnerable may have a strong dislike for people speaking to them with their hands in their faces. Even a slight gesture could signal a fight or flight response. When the arms are thrusting forward, this is a scare tactic usually intended to create emphasis. We fight with our arms and hands, so the connection between the two is threatening.

When the arms are positioned behind the backs and out of sight of the person they are engaging with, this indicates hidden intent. The person may lack confidence, or they are attempting to hide their fear through fiddling with their hands behind their backs. This isn't necessarily a sign of a liar. Rather, the person may simply feel uncomfortable, or they are preventing themselves from saying something.

The elbows, when facing out, could be a silent cry for space. A person may want others to back away from them without having to actually verbally express their disposition. This can easily be observed through the actions of children. Toddlers, who cannot communicate verbally, will often extend their elbows in a sharp motion in order to indicate space. As adults, we do this subconsciously as a means of inner protection.

The hands are quite detailed in their means of communication. One move of the hand can indicate an invitation while another movement could ignite conflict. When the hands are crossed with the thumbs tucked under, this is a signal of peace. East Indian gurus can be seen holding their hands in this way to express giving, peaceful natures. They wish to extend this light to others through their physical movements. When the hands are placed in front of the belly button, with the fingers touching and open palms, this is a symbol of dignity. The person is trying to show their partner that they are confident, professional, and conscientious.

The hands are also key indicators of direction. We use our fingers to point towards areas of interest. When the hands are placed delicately on the knees with the palms down, this could indicate submission, especially when leaning towards the opposite person. Women usually engage in this stance while attempting to show interest in a flirtatious manner. Hand gestures can also indicate movement. When the palm is facing a person, this translates to dismissal and disapproval. The person is using their hands to physically block the other person from their sight.

When the hands are touching parts of the face, this could translate to brainstorming, boredom, or even decision making. When the palms are essentially holding the face and cheeks upward, this is a clear indicator of a person attempting to wake themselves up from a boring situation. It shows disinterest in the most obvious of ways. However, when the index finger is pointing towards certain areas of the face, a person could be deep in thought.

The positioning of the fingers as well as the firmness of their grasp is telling.

Excessive shaking that permeates throughout the palms and into the fingers occurs during high stress situations. A person may be so nervous, their hands begin to shake uncontrollably. This also is a sign of intense hunger. The hands and fingers begin to grow unsteady, thus displaying the body's lack of food. Slight trembles can also occur when a person is being caught in a lie or confronted for a mistake. They may be so angry that the shakes are their way of expressing that anger.

We use our hands to describe the size and stature of certain things. Much like the arms, they are used to accentuate the gravity of a story, describe the weightiness of a subject, and even demonstrate movement. They are our primary way of gesturing, and they can add great excitement to a story or a conversation. When working together with the arms, the hands can be a great indicator of a person's confidence. Touching creates a sense of warmth and community that connects people together. When analyzed carefully, the movement of the hands and arms can tell us key clues about a person's disposition.

Chapter 10: How to Spot a Lie - Key Behavior that Indicates Deception

Detecting deceit will give you the rare opportunity to choose your associates wisely without having to say a word. The body goes into an immense ball of anxiety when a person lies. The trained eye will be able to detect these small variances that occur. Although words may speak their version of the truth, the body never lies. Deceit is the act of covering up the way you truly feel through seeking control. Oftentimes, that control is executed in a sloppy manner, thus leading to dominant cues that signal deceit. Whether it's a large lie or a little white lie, the results of dishonesty come with a variety of consequences. Essentially, people lie as a subconscious form of protection. They are either hiding their negative behavior or protecting their reputations. Even when used to exaggerate a story, they may be attempting to protect the fact that their life is truly boring. They want others to find them enjoyable. Thus, various lies are told.

One organization divides deceit into four categories of explanation and uses:

Anxiety- seeking to hide the fact that they are nervous

Control- gestures or smiles that are forced or a grand attempt to stop the body from moving

Distraction- Frequent pausing or bodily actions in between answers is that person's attempt to distract you from their lie. By acting out these grand gestures, they believe they are making their stories believable.

Persuasion- Deceit may stem from wanting someone to carry out an action which will result in the liar's favor.

Joseph Tecce, a researcher at Boston College, exposed the six reasons why individuals lie in addition to their respective character traits:

1. Protective Lies: This protects the reputation of the liar or even the victim from undue harm. They seek to keep their social status by not revealing true behavior.

2. Heroic Liars: These individuals will lie in an attempt to uphold the greater good. For example, a popular episode of *Sex and the City* portrayed Carrie and her friend, Stanford, at a mixer. Stanford was interested in a handsome man across the room. He asked Carrie to go and find out if the man was gay or straight. She approached him and let him

know of Stanford's interest. The man looked at Stanford from across the room in utter repulsion. As Carrie went back to her hopeful friend, she told him that the handsome man was straight. She wanted to protect her friend's self-esteem by not revealing the truth.

3. Playful Liars: Playful liars accentuate their stories in order to provide a means of entertainment for listeners.

4. Ego Liars: Ego liars will cover mistakes in order to protect their reputations or status.

5. Gainful Liars: These are people who lie for personal gain.

6. Malicious Liars: These are the individuals who are out to seek revenge and harm others due to psychological challenges.

Many individuals are so crafty at lying; they have mastered the art of concealing their body movements. Sociopaths and psychopaths alike are so deranged; they feel no emotional connection to the lies. It is quite difficult to detect their inaccuracies because they are so connected to the lies. They may even begin to believe the lies. When considering the deceit of mentally stable individuals, however, there may be concrete reasons behind their excessive lying. Let's consider a few signs of a deceitful person and consider their traits.

The head can offer a slight indication of a person beginning to lie. When being asked a question, a liar tends to quickly move their head prior to responding. Interestingly, the face holds many of the truest signs of deception. We express honest emotions through the theory of timing. Researchers have found that, naturally, we hold our expressions between one and four seconds. When a person is lying or faking an emotion, the expression is usually held for a longer period of time. In addition, their symmetrical alignment can play a huge role in detecting insincerity. To tell if a person is being honest, notice the purest emotions are evenly distributed throughout the face. However, a liar will typically express their emotions on one side dominantly. Our speech and body movements should complement each other. So if a person is telling you how beautiful you look while frowning and crossing their arms, it is safe to conclude that they aren't genuine.

Excessive body movements are often associated with nervousness. Naturally, though, the body engages in slight movements even without the presence of anxiety. However, Dr. Leanne Brinke, professor of the Haas School of Business, indicates that a person who remains as still as a statue should be further examined. She says, "You should be just as wary of those who do not move at all as this may be related to the human 'fight or flight' instinct, specifically the option to 'fight.' As a result of this instinct, the body tenses itself in preparation for potential confrontation." Have you ever noticed that when catching someone in a lie, their body tends to freeze almost like a deer caught in headlights? Essentially, they are shocked that their behavior has been caught. At that moment, they have lost all control, and they feel exposed. In order to gain some form of control, they clench their body.

It is also key to notice where their hands go when being confronted. Do they cover their mouths? Throats? Chests? By providing this subtle distraction, they are protecting themselves from the truth. They have no intention of telling the truth, so they are, in effect, covering areas of the body that assist with communication. In addition, verbal cues also point towards deception. Excessive repeating, stuttering, and clearing of the throat are key signs of nervousness. They are desperately trying to buy time to respond.

Traditionally, the eyes have been closely associated with deceit. Previously, we spoke about the connection between dilation and interest. When we see something we love or are attracted to, our eyes dilate. When in a relationship, a key indicator of a loss of interest rests in the pupils. When you ask your mate if your outfit looks great, they may say it looks awesome, but the pupils tell the truth. Excessive darting of the eyes or an avoidance of eye contact signifies some level of deceit. The person may be attempting to put on the demeanor of aggression, but they refuse to look at another's eyes. Are they truly as tough as they say they are? Interestingly, the right side of the brain controls auditory processing, big picture ideas, and decision making. When a person darts their eyes downward and towards the right, they are attempting to envision something, perhaps visiting a place they have never been. They may look down and to the right when thinking about what it's like to live there. When someone is lying, notice how they may repeat this same motion. Interestingly, they are attempting to envision something that didn't occur rather than recall a memory.

The body is also a clear indicator of deceit. You may notice the person's breathing patterns significantly speed up. Their chest could move faster, and their breathing becomes louder. Their shoulders and elbows are stiffly raised. This movement represents being caught, as seen depicted in cartoons. The robber may inadvertently stop in their tracks with their shoulders raised. They are trying to protect themselves by growing defensive. Psychics and spiritual healers utilize exposed palms to reveal truth. Although controversial, many readers analyze the open palms to detect repressed emotions, predict future occurrences, and decode personality. When a person is lying, those palms of truth are suddenly closed and facing away from the subject. It's a subconscious way of not wanting to reveal their truth.

Although detecting liars is an essential tool to have, simply noticing a liar isn't productive. Effective communication in conjunction with understanding can help to reveal lies and reach solutions.

Chapter 11: How to Spot Romantic Interest - Body Language Cues that Signal Attraction

Being able to detect if a person is truly into you can save a lot of time and heartache when dating. There are specific body movements that are unique to men and women that display attraction. Sure, words are powerful, but actions are groundbreaking. This form of body language is the most sensual in nature and inviting. Many of the common depictions on cartoons and illustrations are quite accurate when it comes to flirting. Women have a unique set of body language cues that are attractive to men. It complements their feminine role and can be used as a form of luring the man in. Men demonstrate a similar display of body cues that align with their masculinity. Oftentimes, the cues are so strong, they release certain hormones related to sexual attraction. The act of engaging in sexual pleasure is body language at its height. Since words are not commonly used as a sexual act, intercourse is the purest form of visually displaying that attraction. However, the journey from first date to the bedroom is filled with subtle clues that could alter the destination. Let's consider the primary difference between men and women when it comes to displaying attraction.

Women

When a woman finds a male attractive, she may begin by locking eyes with him. She could give a subtle gaze and then look away. If this continues, the woman essentially wants the man to chase her. Simple touches to the body and even her curling her hair with fingers are used to flirt. This brings attention to the feminine qualities of a woman that may be attractive to the man. When a woman raises her eyebrows when talking with a man, they are signaling attraction. She may find the man to be physically handsome or admirable. Or she may be so caught up in what he is saying that it moves her to agree. The lips also indicate attraction especially in the biting, licking, or caressing them. When a woman looks intently at a man's lips and then makes direct eye contact, this is a subconscious invitation to kiss.

As mentioned previously, women tend to lean in toward their dates to show attraction. When her legs are crossed inward, facing her date, it's a suggestive pose that indicates sexual interest. This is heightened when the genitals are exposed and involve a light caress. Women may also arch their backs to further elongate their spines. The curvature of their spine is a feminine quality that is attractive to the man. Slight exposure of the breast is a sign of intense flirtation. She is drawing the man into her womanhood to express interest.

Women may also "bat" their eyes up and down rapidly as a sign of flirtation. This brings attention to the lashes which, when elongated, are physically pleasing to the man. She may pair this with a slight giggle to signal attraction.

Oftentimes, women tend to "mirror" the movements of men. This signifies submission as the woman is showing respect for the position of the man. Inadvertently, she is following the lead of her date. Many sensual dances rely on the man leading and the woman following. Women subconsciously perform these acts as a means to show respect for the men's masculinity.

Men

When a man moves his head slightly, raises his brows, and allows his nostrils to flare, he is indicating attraction. When paired with a smile, the level of attraction is heightened. Initially, a man will avoid making direct eye contact as he may be nervous or unaware of the woman's attraction level. In addition, men speak with their chest. If the chest is pointing towards the woman, he is giving her his full attention. If his chest is pointing elsewhere, he secretly wants to escape the situation.

Men want to appear dominant, masculine, and strong to perspective dates. They may stand with their feet wide and their hands on their hips in order to appear sturdy. If his hands are gracing his waist line, he essentially wants the woman to look near his genitals. This is a silent invitation to a possible sexual encounter. Men tend to show their attraction through their hands. Slight touches to the back, thigh, and arm indicates sexual attraction. However, a pat on the shoulder could be read as platonic.

There are universal signs of attraction carried out by both men and women. Smiling and a willingness to laugh without apprehension are valuable signs. Spatial awareness is a key indicator to revealing intent. When two people are attracted to each other, they tend to stand close. Their shoulders are raised and positioned inwardly which indicates interest. Even the positioning of the toes symbolizes attraction. As mentioned, the toes point to where they want to go. When the toes are facing each other, sometimes called "pigeon toed," they are subtle signs of flirting. The man or woman wants to appear cute and coy. This vulnerable position subconsciously boosts sexual attraction. The palms traditionally reveal truth. When a man or a woman is interested, their palms may rest in an exposed position. It promotes openness which indicates that the two would like to get to know each other.

The laws of attraction are traditional as they signify small psychological changes that are quite universal. When a person speaks their intent with body language cues to follow, you can guarantee their validity. By understanding these simple cues, you will be better equipped to make accurate perceptions about the intent of others.

Chapter 12: How to Spot Insecurity - Small Signs that Show a Lack of Confidence

When people lack confidence, they display those characteristics boldly. Their posture and demeanor speak volumes so loud; others immediately respond. Unfortunately, these body positions prevent individuals from being treated with respect. They are more susceptible to being taken advantage of, passed up for opportunities, and even disrespected. Why is this the case?

Our brain perceives certain body movements as being weak. Previously, we discussed different body movements that signal submission. While having a submissive personality is generally accepted as being mild, it doesn't equate a lack of confidence. Moreover, the body cues being demonstrated are similar in nature but intricately different. One of the primary indicators of a person lacking self-confidence is engaging in extremes. This can be found when individuals attempt to become "larger than life" by outward displays of dominance. Their initial appearance may seem intimidating, but their core is weak. They exude this fake confidence as a mask to cover up their inner conflict. Obnoxious, loud, domineering, and dismissive gestures are used to compensate for something they are lacking. Whether it's physical beauty, intelligence, or inner insecurities, your untrained eye may view them with admiration, even succumbing to their ploys. Once you are trained, it is quite obvious for you to see through their excessive demeanor.

Posture

A person's posture says a lot about their inward confidence. A tall, relaxed back indicates true confidence. There is nothing forced or excessively pronounced. When a person seems to loom over others with a widened stance, they are seeking authority. They may feel insecure about their current lot in life, so they attempt to make others feel small physically. In addition, slouched shoulders, a downturned chin, and legs close together are obvious signs of insecurity. The way a person positions himself in a chair also speaks volumes. If they are slouched, with arms tightly crossed, they are attempting to protect themselves. They may suffer from social anxiety and seek to disappear.

Eye Contact

As previously mentioned, direct eye contact reveals confidence. When a person avoids making eye contact with someone by looking away or downward, they are secretly wishing to escape. They are fearful of what the other person is thinking, so they retreat to a safe space. You can always tell when someone is forcing eye contact as they blink less frequently in an attempt to control the direction of their eyes. In summation, their gaze isn't natural. It appears forced and likely strange.

Touching the Self

In an attempt to distract themselves from the current situation, insecure people will often fiddle with their teeth, touch their heads, or rub areas of their bodies. This is not an inviting or suggestive means to seduce. Rather, it's a coping mechanism used to calm the body and mind. This is why nail biting is often associated with being nervous.

When individuals constantly fiddle with their clothing or readjust certain aspects of their appearance, they may feel insecure about their outward appearance. They may feel the need to fix themselves in order to fit the expectations of those around them. Oftentimes, people who try out new looks may constantly mess with their clothing because they are not accustomed to the style.

Excessive Movements

Leg, arm, and hand movements indicate nervousness or anxiety. When a person fidgets with different sections of the body, this is another sign of self-soothing. They are nervous about the conversation or even the environment they are in. You may notice that public speakers tend to fiddle with their ring or wrists when speaking about a challenging topic. In addition, placing your hands in your pockets, thus hiding them from the public, is a sign of apprehension. You are sending the message of fear as you are attempting to conceal something.

As mentioned, the reverse is true for individuals who are immensely insecure. They attempt to overcompensate for what they are lacking by relying on superiority. Alfred Adler was a groundbreaking psychologist who studied human behavior. He thoroughly researched what he named the inferiority complex which addresses exaggerated behaviors as a means to gain respect. Adler said people who feel inferior go about their days overcompensating through what he called "striving for superiority." According to the article, "The only way these inwardly uncertain people can feel happy is by making others decidedly unhappy." These individuals may use excessive physical displays of anger as a means to gain control and ignite fear.

The slamming of doors, banging on desks, and even hanging up the phone with force are classic signals. When engaging in conversation, they rarely make eye contact perhaps busying themselves with other tasks. This outright dismissiveness is their way of showing others how important they think they are. On the inside, they may be recovering from past experiences of not being listened to. They may make others feel inferior as a means to seek revenge.

Another sign of insecurity is excessive laughing. As a means to fill the gap of conversation, a person may nervously laugh excessively. They are drastically uncomfortable and are at a loss for words. They may feel that laughing gives them the opportunity to make a fake connection. This could be accompanied by uncomfortable sweating or blushing. The body is physically revealing signs of embarrassment which increases our body temperature. Sweat may begin to lightly appear. The person may even begin to feel increasingly self-conscious about their sweat as well.

In this technology-filled world, cell phones are like extensions of the body. If a person constantly fiddles with their phone during social outings, they are probably suffering from extreme discomfort. They are attempting to calm their nerves through a cell phone screen. They may find scrolling through their social media as a form of comfort as it distracts them from actually engaging in a conversation.

Detecting insecurity isn't meant to give you power over vulnerable individuals. Rather, it is an inward ability to adjust your reactions to their behavior. If you encounter someone who is seeking to overcompensate by making others feel bad, you can detect that and handle them accordingly. You can see past their demeanor and ignore their "threats." When encountering a traditionally insecure person, you will know how to handle them with care. This knowledge will boost your ability to establish successful relationships and even boost social morale.

Conclusion

The body is a fascinating group of systems that work coherently to expose our innermost emotions. From a simple glimpse of the eyes all the way down to the positioning of the toes, the body is honest. Mastering the art of analyzing others begins with a comprehensive understanding of yourself. Even different inflections of the voice can change a sentence in its entirety. In addition, the art of touch can mean the difference between attraction and repulsion. Learning how to analyze others assists with social connection and your ability to understand what others are truly saying. The beauty behind the human connection is that there are universal mannerisms that give off social cues open for interpretation. A simple shrug of the brows paired with a crossing of the arms signals a sign of discontent. A slight lean inward can give you the signal that your date is legitimately into you! These subtle cues are intricate in nature, but the magnitude is revolutionary. By mastering these techniques, you will have this unwavering gift that is easily applicable to your everyday life. You will be able to seek the truth and defend yourself against possible threats. One of the key secrets to mastering the art of analyzing others is keying in on your observation skills. The entire body works in conjunction with the brain to send and expel certain messages that define emotions, often leading to subconscious visual cues that may give away the true thoughts and feelings of a given individual without their even realizing what they are doing. Inside, you will find dozens of different ways to pick up on those cues for fun and profit. By being observant and truly reading the behaviors of others, you will be able to emphasize this gift to meet your needs. We encourage you to implement these practices into your daily life to further analyze yourself and truly be able to read others.

The next step is to practice these tips throughout your daily life! By doing so, you will gain a better understanding of yourself and human behavior as a whole.

Manipulation

The Complete Psychologist's Guide to Highly Effective Manipulation and Deception Techniques – Influence People with NLP, Mind Control and Persuasion

Introduction

While our lives might look all great and beautiful on the outside with an ideal upbringing, great education and a stellar career, we've all been victims of unsavory tactics used by people to have their way by preying on our feelings, self-worth and emotions.

We've all been part of manipulative relationships where the strings of our feelings and emotions were cleverly controlled by another person to fulfill their needs.

While humans at large thrive on love, kindness and gratitude, it cannot be denied that it can be a self-centered species at times. Yes, we can be self-serving by nature! You may not think being selfish or self-serving is a negative trait. Why shouldn't we think about ourselves? However, some folks take this self-centeredness too far. In their bid to serve their needs, they tread upon the feelings and emotions of others.

When people start resorting to intentional, calculated and cunning techniques for having their way, this is what makes it harmful and immoral. The intensity of this may vary from person to person depending on their upbringing, environment, personality, experiences, education and several other factors.

We all are guilty of using manipulation at some point, often without realizing it. In the same vein, we are often manipulated by people close to us without realizing that we are being victims of manipulation. And this is precisely what makes it so sinister and insidious. We are made to think, feel and act in a specific way to fulfill another person's need without consideration for our emotions.

For instance, you may be made to feel guilty about working hard or putting in long hours of work even though you are doing it to build a future for your loved ones. Or you'll be made to feel like you are an irresponsible person for taking a break from housework and letting yourself have fun with friends.

The stark reality about manipulation is that it originates from people who are grappling with issues related to security, self-confidence and comfort. They attempt to push their luck in a bid to hold other people down for fear of losing them. Manipulators operate from a deep sense of insecurity. Ironically, what they don't realize is that, in their bid to hold people down owing to the fear of losing them, they end up doing just that - losing people!

Other times, manipulators are simply out to take advantage of people to serve their cut throat, selfish purposes. They are cold, calculating and ruthless in their acts. There is no regard for the feelings and emotions of their victims. It is a 'dog-eat-dog' world according to them, and to survive, they believe they have to use other people.

Manipulators operate with a point of view that they must reach their end through whatever means it takes, and if it ends up hurting a few people along the way, so be it. These are people you should actively watch out for and avoid.

The purpose of this book is to make you aware of the sneaky tricks people use for manipulating others. It aims to uncover how people use emotional manipulation, mind control and persuasion to fulfill their own needs.

When you are able to identify clever manipulative techniques, it becomes easier to guard against them. You'll learn to read warning signs of manipulation and use practical techniques to safeguard your emotions and self-confidence, thus accomplishing complete immunity against people's sly tactics.

Chapter 1: Examining Emotional Manipulation

Have you lost count of the number of times you've been told, that if you love someone, you will or won't do something for them? Why do people equate an emotion like love with such frivolous matters as grabbing dinner at a particular restaurant or catching a new release movie? Well, that is the power of emotions. Emotions are a double-edged sword that can be leveraged both positively and negatively by people for fulfilling their needs.

During the 20th century, one of the planet's most powerful leaders recognized the power of emotions on people. He devoted years to getting the finer nuances of body language right by analyzing visuals of his posture, expressions, hand gestures and more. He mastered the art of spellbinding, almost hypnotizing, people through his public speeches and gestures. His name: Adolf Hitler.

The last thing you want is to be emotionally manipulated by everyone from your friends to co-workers to politicians to your partner. People using manipulation may knowingly or unknowingly disregard ethics and prey on your emotions to serve their needs.

While each of us is guilty of using manipulation (knowingly or unknowingly) at some point, what makes emotional manipulators different is they habitually trample upon people's emotions and feelings to serve their own selfish needs. It is a way of life for some people to use other people's feelings in a bid to increase their psychological hold or superiority over the person.

Manipulation is starkly different from persuasion. While persuasion awards the other person a right to select his/her response to a particular situation, manipulation does not give the victim the right to choose. Manipulation has only one way – the way your manipulator wants you to take. There is only one single 'correct choice': the manipulator's choice. There is zero regard or concern for your wishes, desires, choices and emotions. You will pay with hell if you don't pick the choice they want you to.

Typical manipulative tactics include:

- Complaining
- Playing victim
- Inducing guilt
- Comparing
- Offering excuses and rationalizing
- Feigning ignorance
- Emotional blackmail
- Evasiveness
- Demonstrating fake concern
- Undermining people

- Blaming others and using "Who me?" defenses
- Lying
- Denying
- False flattery
- Intimidation
- Giving the illusion of selflessness
- Shaming

Using foot in the door techniques

Here are different ways through which we experience emotional manipulation in our lives (and you may not have even been aware you were being manipulated):

1. Emotional manipulators play on people's fears. Emotional manipulators tend to blow facts out of proportion and highlight only specific points in a bid to instill fear in you. For example, a man who doesn't want his wife to pursue a full-time career outside the house may tell her something like, "Research reveals 60 percent of all divorces happen when both partners are engaged in full-time careers," sneakily hiding the fact that there can be reasons other than the woman's career or job.

This is cleverly constructed to prey on the woman's fear of losing the relationship as she gives in to her ambitions.

2. The actions and words of emotional manipulators seldom match. Emotional manipulators tell you exactly what they think you

want to hear but will rarely follow it up with action. They will pledge commitment and support. However, when it comes to acting upon their commitment, they will make you feel guilty for coming up with unreasonable demands.

At one point, they'll tell you how fortunate they are to know a person like you, and the next they'll be slamming you for being a burden. This is a clever tactic for undermining your own belief about your sanity. Emotional manipulators will keep saying things that suit their purpose and suddenly mold a perception to the contrary by doing the opposite of what they said to misbalance your sanity.

Their help also comes at a price, which they'll sneakily claim in the future. They will constantly remind you of how they helped you and use that as a leverage to get you to feel obliged to them. If you are perpetually being reminded of a favor they willingly did for you, which makes you feel you owe them something, there are high chances you are being emotionally manipulated.

3. They are masters at distributing guilt. Few people leverage the power of guilt like practiced manipulators. Emotional manipulators induce guilt in other people to serve their needs. If you bring up an issue for discussion that's been bothering you, they'll make you feel guilty about feeling the way you do, however justified your feelings are. Emotional manipulators will make you feel guilty for mentioning the issue. When you don't mention

the issue, they'll make you feel miserable for not being open and talking about it.

All they do is keep stewing guilt in you, irrespective of the direction of your thoughts and actions. One way or another, they'll find reasons to make you feel guilty. When you are with an emotional manipulator, anything you choose to do is wrong. Irrespective of the problems you may be having collectively, an emotional manipulator will always make you feel it is only your fault. They will blame you for everything unfortunate happening in their life and build a strong sense of guilt within you.

4. They'll don the victim's role. Where emotional manipulation is concerned, nothing that happens is ever their mistake. Irrespective of their actions, they will always blame someone else for their failings.

They'll often harp on how they were made to do something by you. If you get angry or hurt, you are the one responsible for building unreasonable expectations. If they get angry or upset, you are responsible for hurting them. There is zero accountability for any action.

For example, if a person forgets their partner's birthday, and the partner gets upset about it, they'll generally apologize and promise to make good for it in future. However, an emotionally manipulative person will not just deny it is their fault; they will also make their partner feel miserable for blaming them.

They will go off about how stressed they've been of late, owing it to something the partner has done, that it's just impossible for them to remember it. The manipulator will go a step ahead and remind you of instances where you've forgotten something important to justify their fault.

5. Emotional manipulators expect too much, way too soon. From an interpersonal relationship to a business association, emotional manipulators are always moving in very fast, while overlooking a few steps along the way. They may share too much too early in a relationship and expect the other person to do the same.

Their vulnerability, transparency and sensitivity are a clever ruse. This is a 'special' charade to make you feel a part of their inner circle. Slowly and insidiously, you'll not just feel sorry about their feelings but also responsible for them.

6. Emotional manipulators belittle your faith in understanding reality. These people, you must hand it to them, are exceptionally skilled liars and cheats. They will confidently insist something happened when it didn't and deny it happened when it did. They do this in such a devious and underhanded manner that you begin questioning your own sanity.

For example, if you suspect your partner of having an affair and confront them about it, the emotionally manipulative partner will outright deny it (even though it is the truth), and in turn make you feel like an insane, suspicious person who doesn't have a grip on reality.

Even though your suspicion is not unfounded, you'll be made to feel guilty about spying around and not trusting your partner. It'll come to a point where you will begin questioning your own suspicious nature and sanity. I am sure many of you are nodding your head in agreement to this!

I know by now you've already identified such people and relationships. I have, and imagine, we weren't even aware of these snarky, insidious tactics when we were being manipulated.

7. Everyone must feel the way they do. Wow, this is another sneaky emotional manipulation technique used to suck other people into their emotional state. The emotional manipulator wants everyone to feel the way they are feeling. If they are in a foul mood, everyone around should be aware of it.

However, it doesn't end there. Not only should everyone know how they are feeling, they should also be sucked into the emotional state of the manipulator. Whatever other people are feeling or experiencing should be dropped , and they should instantly match the emotional frequency of the manipulator. This makes people around them feel like they are responsible for the emotional manipulator's feelings, and they alone should fix it.

8. Eagerness to help becomes a burden later. Emotional manipulators will volunteer to help initially (and pretty eagerly at that) only to make

themselves look like martyrs later. They will act like what they initially agreed to do is a huge burden.

If you remind them that they committed to the task, they'll turn around and make you feel like a paranoid person despite them appearing eager to help. The objective? To induce a feeling of guilt, feeling obliged towards them and probably even questioning your sanity!

9. One-upmanship games. Irrespective of the intensity of your problems and challenges, the manipulator will always make it come across as their problems are much worse. They will attempt to undermine the authenticity of your problems by constantly reinforcing how much bigger their problems or challenges are.

They'll make you feel guilty for complaining about 'trivial' things when they are facing serious issues. The goal? You don't have any reason to complain about your 'non-serious' problems, while they have every right to keep reminding you of their 'serious' problems. In other words, they want you to shut up and stop complaining about your problems, so they will always be one-up in every situation.

10. They know your emotional buttons and how to press them at will. We all have our emotional weak spots. Emotional manipulators are cleverly aware of your weak spots and do not hesitate to use them for serving their own sinister objectives. They will use knowledge of your weak spots against you.

For example, if you are insecure about your appearance, they will pass snide remarks about everything from your clothes to your weight. Again, if you are worried about an upcoming speech, they will prey on your fears by telling you how tough, picky and judgmental the audience is. They use awareness of your emotions not to make you feel better, but to manipulate you into feeling worse.

11. Emotional manipulators use humor to take a dig at your perceived weaknesses to disempower you or make you feel inadequate. Notice how some people are perpetually making critical or snide remarks about their partner or friend, often in the garb of humor. The idea is to make the other person feel inadequate, inferior or insecure.

Emotional manipulators attempt to disempower the person by playing on his/her perceived weaknesses. The remarks encompass everything from the person's appearance to their old phone to their skills. They make sarcastic and seemingly funny comments about everything, including the fact that you walked in 30 seconds late.

The idea is to make you look bad and feel worse about yourself. This way, the manipulator tries to gain psychological dominance over you, unfortunately, without you even realizing it (now you do, right?). Undermining you makes you perceive yourself as inferior, which automatically gives them the much-needed psychological superiority.

12. Emotional manipulators constantly judge and criticize you to make you feel inferior. In the above example, we saw how manipulators use covert techniques to disempower you by disguising their snide remarks as humor. However, here the emotional manipulator outright dismisses, marginalizes, criticizes and ridicules you in a bid to maintain psychological superiority over you.

Their premise is, if they make you feel inadequate and off-balance, their chances of getting you to do whatever they want increase. You will stop believing in your abilities, sanity and worth, which will help them wield greater control over your thoughts, emotions and actions.

The emotional aggressor will intentionally foster the feeling that something is not right with you, and that, however hard you try, you won't be good enough. Significantly, the emotional manipulator will emphasize on the weaknesses without offering constructive or positive solutions or assisting you in meaningful ways to overcome the negatives.

13. Emotional manipulators will give you the silent treatment. Another art emotional manipulators have mastered is the art of giving people the silent treatment to pressure them into doing what the manipulator wants. They will intentionally make you wait and sow seeds of doubt, insecurity and uncertainty in your mind. Emotional manipulators use silence as leverage to get you to do what they want by keeping you emotionally deprived or insecure.

Being at the receiving end of silent treatment is a warning sign you are dealing with an emotional manipulator. It is a type of emotional abuse through which contempt is demonstrated through nonverbal acts such as remaining silent or withdrawing all communication.

The silent treatment is used as a tool to incite their victims into doing something specific or make them feel inadequate by refusing to acknowledge their presence. If your actions don't match what the manipulator wants you to do, they will utilize the silent treatment for communicating their disappointment and punishing you.

14. Pretend play. Yes, they can play dumb, too, whenever needed. They will pretend that they don't understand what exactly you want or what you desire from them. This is one of the sneaky passive-aggressive tricks where their responsibility becomes yours. So, the bonus of what is essentially their responsibility is thrown on your shoulders. This is often used by people who are trying to hide something or avoid an obligation.

15. Raising voice and demonstrating negative emotions. Some emotional manipulators know how to use the power of their voice and body language to coerce you into meeting their demands.

They will often raise their voice as a type of aggressive manipulation with the belief that if they sound intimidating enough with their voice, tone and body language, you will invariably submit to their demands. The aggressor-like voice is often combined with intimidating body language such as exaggerated gestures and standing to increase the effect of their aggressive manipulative actions.

16. Negative surprises as a norm. Whoa! Don't these people know how to throw you off balance with their negative surprises in an obvious attempt to gain a psychological advantage over you? They will suddenly come up with some information about not being able to do something or deliver a commitment as promised.

Typically, the negative information is thrown on you without any forewarning to catch you off guard. You are left with no time to come up with a counter move. Emotional manipulators are wolves in sheep's clothing and won't spare a single opportunity to cause discomfort, hurt or harm to you if you get in the way.

Chapter 2: Tips for Spotting Covert Manipulation Techniques

Recognizing covert manipulation tactics is tricky because, unlike overt manipulation, these aren't obvious or in your face. They are often underhanded techniques of trying to gain control of the victim's thoughts, feelings and decisions. It is aimed at bringing down a person's sense of self-worth and destroying their belief in their perceptions. When you learn the manipulator's game, you can play it better than them.

Manipulation undermines the victim's ability to make conscious decisions and act in accordance with their interests. Instead, they become mere puppets in someone else's hands. Manipulators don't value people's personal values, desires and boundaries. In plain words, they'll make you do something you wouldn't normally do.

So, what are the most widely used covert manipulation tactics, and how do you spot them in your everyday life? Read on to de-bluff people's covert manipulation games.

1. They will create a false sense of intimacy. Notice how people are constantly sharing intimate information about themselves in the early stages of a relationship? They will talk about their family,

backgrounds and lives (often portraying themselves as victims of circumstances) in a bid to win your sympathy, while also creating an illusion of intimacy.

2. They will introduce other people in the picture in a bid to make you insecure. Again, some people are always trying to create a sense of insecurity or discomfort in their victims by introducing other people into the picture. For example, your partner may talk about meeting an ex-girlfriend/boyfriend or good friend to make you feel insecure.

Of course, not everyone who meets friends or ex-partners is being manipulative. However, covert manipulators are constantly using this tactic of introducing other people into the picture to unsettle their partner. When a person is trying to pit other people against you to make you feel inadequate, you can be sure it's a covert manipulation tactic.

3. Another covert manipulation technique is 'foot in the door', which is fairly easy to recognize. It involves making a small request that the victim agrees to, which is subsequently followed by the actual intended request. It is tougher to refuse once the victim agrees to the initial request.

If you refuse the actual request, you'll come across as someone who agrees to something they don't intend to do. When you object to the real request, the manipulator will quickly turn the tables to come across as the aggrieved party. It stops being about their demands since they are now the injured ones. The focus shifts to their complaints, and you are placed on the defensive now. Sometimes, warnings and worry about your well-being are cleverly hidden as concern. Manipulators are forever trying to undermine your choices and decisions in an attempt to shake your self-confidence or sense of self-worth.

4. "Snakes in Suits" – In their publication *Snakes in Suits,* Robert Hare and Paul Babaik advise how people should guard against manipulators who offer out of place and excessive compliments. It is a huge manipulation red flag. Focus keenly on what's next. Keep questioning yourself, *What exactly does this person want from me?*

5. Force Teaming. Have you noticed how some people are always creating a forced sense of team spirit or shared purpose where none exists? Typical phrases used by them include, "We're one team," "How do we handle this as a team?" "We've done it now," etc. They purportedly try to portray that you both are involved in something as a team.

In such a situation, how can you tell if the person is being genuinely helpful or simply trying to manipulate you? Do you feel a strange sense of discomfort while accepting their help? Are their words congruent with their body language? (More on body language later). Is the person giving you an option to refuse help? Are they taking your refusal in the right spirit? If no, you may be dealing with a covert manipulator who is trying to manipulate you under the guise of offering you help.

6. **Flattering First Impression.** Practiced manipulators often make a stellar first impression. They use a bunch of enticing characteristics such as flawless manners, attractive looks, charismatic smile and courtesy to throw their victims off guard about their real intentions. Yes, they exist beyond the movies, where con men and women are shown to be these stereotypical characters with a dazzling personality and a glib tongue.

With manipulators, what appears on the surface is not the truth. However, with time and observation, you will notice the cracks in their cleverly worn masks. When it gets really sadistic, the silence is used to torture their victims. For instance, a co-worker talks to everyone at work but ignores you or refuses to have any conversation with you.

7. Covert manipulators will appear to be selfless by keeping their real intentions, ambitions, goals and agendas cleverly cloaked. Their true intentions are hidden under the garb of a selfless cause. This one's tricky to identify. These are the people who will act like they are working hard on behalf of another person, while hiding their true ambition for power and dominance over others.

For example, a covert manipulator will give his/her manager the impression that they are willing to put in extra hours of work when the manager is away on vacation only to fulfill their ambition of eventually taking over the manager's position.

8. Gas Lighting. The term gas lighting as a covert manipulation technique comes from the play of the same name, which was later adapted into films. It has also been used in literature and psychological research.

Using the gas lighting technique, a manipulator will twist reality to fulfill their objectives. Irrespective of the truth, they have tricks up their sleeves for making you think that it is indeed your fault for not being able to perceive things correctly. It is so deeply ingrained into your mind that you stop trusting your perceptions and instead accept the manipulator's contrived version of truth. The technique is intended to make you feel so mentally incompetent that you stop trusting your version of reality. It gets to a point where if someone tries to challenge your perceptions, you are mistrustful of them.

9. Rationalization. Rationalization is a technique through which a manipulator offers some form of justification for a hurtful, offensive or inappropriate action. What makes the technique so tough to spot is that the explanation given often contains enough sense for any reasonable individual to buy it.

Rationalization fulfills three fundamental purposes including, eliminating resistance that manipulators may have about their inappropriate action, keeping others from pointing fingers at them and helping the manipulator justify his/her actions in the victim's eyes.

Manipulators who use rationalization will typically behave very affectionately at times and then suddenly act distant or cold. When the victim gets tired of their behavior and confronts them or avoids them, they will most likely scream or cry. They will mention how they have been depressed or upset of late and how you are such a bad person for confronting them about their seemingly inappropriate behavior when you are one who is behaving insensitively.

They will move you to tears with how stressful their life is, even apologize for it at times. However, within the next few days, they'll repeat the pattern. Manipulators are remarkable performers. They can play the victim's role with ease. They can fake emotions, cry at will, laugh when they want to and pretend to be sad or happy on demand. Carefully examine the acts of people who 'love you' or forever try to gain sympathy.

10. Nitpicking and goal post moving. The difference between positive criticism and negative/destructive criticism is a manipulator will come up with near impractical standards and personal attacks. These self-proclaimed critics pretend to help your development, when in fact, they don't want to see you improve. They are simply operating with the intention of nitpicking at

you, pulling you down and making you a scapegoat in every possible manner.

Covert manipulators are masters in the art of 'moving goalposts' to ensure they are never short of reasons to be disappointed with you. Even when you present evidence to validate your stand or act to fulfill their request, they will come up with another lofty expectation for you to meet or ask for more proof to validate your argument. Yes, who said dealing with manipulators was easy?

For example, they may start by picking on you for not having a successful career. When you have a successful career, they'll question you for not being a multi-millionaire yet. When that expectation is met, they'll demand to know why your personal/work life is never balanced. The goal posts will keep changing, and the expectations will rise higher in a bid to make you feel incompetent in some way or the other.

One of the easiest ways to spot a manipulator is to observe if they are constantly instilling a sense of unworthiness in you or forever making you feel whatever you do is never good enough. A genuine or constructive person will never induce a sense of unworthiness in you. They will gently point out your limitations and often suggest ways to overcome them. Manipulators, on the other hand, will never offer suggestions to help you overcome your limitations.

If a person is constantly criticizing you without helping you overcome the issue or limitations in a meaningful way, you may likely be a victim of covert manipulation. They will cleverly present it as constructive criticism even if it's just nitpicking without offering solutions.

If a person keeps demanding more proof for validating your argument or keeps raising their expectations, their aim is obviously not to understand you better. They are attempting to provoke you into experiencing a sense of inadequacy or that you have to keep proving yourself all the time.

11. Withholding apology. Covert manipulators will seldom apologize for their actions. Instead they will deny, lie or shift the blame to avoid accepting responsibility for their act. Be mindful of this covert manipulation technique by examining if the person apologizes and accepts responsibility for their mistakes.

If a person constantly makes you feel like you are blowing things out of proportion or overreacting rather than apologizing, you are probably dealing with a covert manipulator. Manipulators have a strong urge to be right, even at the cost of mending a relationship. Withholding apology is just another controlling mechanism for them.

12. Undermining your success. I once had a friend who was constantly made to feel guilty by his partner about being successful. He was creating a

promising future for them and their future kids, but she constantly made him feel terrible about the fact that he worked so hard and barely had time for her. She accused him of being selfish and thinking only about his goals, when in fact, he was building a future for their family.

When you tell your partner or a close friend about a promotion or a new job offer, how should they usually react? They should be delighted you are progressing in life. Those who truly care about you will want to see you succeed. Manipulators will constantly try to underplay and undermine your success. They will always find some way to instill negativity in any form related to your success story. This arises from a clear sense of insecurity that you are now becoming more self-sufficient and will no longer need them.

The feeling that the more successful you become, the less they'll be able to control you leads them to behave in an irrational manner. Thus, they'll make you feel miserable about your success. Sometimes, they'll even get angry for no apparent reason. One of their biggest concerns is that financial independence will give you the ability to survive without their help. This prospect can be threatening for a person who is accustomed to having his/her friend or partner depend on him/her excessively.

Chapter 3: Why Manipulators Manipulate

Now that you are fairly competent in identifying emotional and covert manipulation tactics, let's understand what leads people to manipulate others. This may help you deal with them more efficiently.

We've all been victims of everything from pathological lying to being made to feel inadequate to suffering awful smear campaigns. They are beyond reasonable standards of human behavior. What makes people turn into sinister manipulators? What leads manipulators to use the tactics they do? What makes them defy norms of human behavior and turn to underhanded techniques to have their way with people?

Read on to get deeper insights about what makes people manipulate others in ways you'd never imagine.

Fear

Why does a person use manipulation to fulfill his/her own agenda? Simple - fear!

It is obvious that manipulators fear that they will never be able to gain the desired outcome on their own abilities. That if they act ethically, people and life will not reward them positively. They operate from the view that people are life, and people are positioned against them. Manipulators fear everyone as their enemy and believe life will not necessarily be favorable to them if they act favorably.

There is a fear that resources are limited, and if they don't gain something, others will. They think it's a dog-eat-dog universe where people must be controlled to help them accomplish the desired result. This control can be in any form – emotional, psychological, financial or practical. They want to control people, so they can achieve their desired agenda and put their fear to rest.

Manipulators are constantly living under fear and insecurity. 'What if this doesn't happen?' 'What if my partner leaves me for someone else?' 'What if someone gains an upper hand over me?' They want to win and control all the time to combat an inherent sense of fear.

Where does this fear stem from? It originates from a deep sense of unworthiness. This simply translates as 'I am certainly not worthy of the good things and people in life, hence, these things and people will leave me. To prevent them from leaving me, I must resort to some underhanded techniques that will give me absolute control over the people and things I believe I don't deserve.' In short, the underlying message is – 'I am undeserving or unworthy of people and things!'

Low or No Conscience

Lack of conscience is another fundamental reason for manipulation. When a person fails to realize that he/she is responsible for their own reality, there is a greater tendency to operate without a conscience. Manipulators don't believe a fair system exists. Also, they've stopped evolving. They don't learn from earlier experiences or try to accomplish a state of congruence between inner emotions and external life.

They view manipulation as a safe or secure world for getting the desired result, despite the fact that these results have not brought them satisfaction in the past. Emotionally and psychologically, they keep coming back to square one from time to time, never learning their lesson. To avoid this lesson, they will create another reason to manipulate. Thus, they are caught in vicious circle of unworthiness or dissatisfaction, thus, creating another manipulation need.

Manipulation doesn't pay beyond the initial brief fix since the manipulative action is not authentic, balanced or effective. It is a defense reaction to perceived hurt, unworthiness, fear or insecurity. By being manipulative, the person is attempting to offset these emotions.

Manipulation is a deliberate act that is not aligned with a person's conscience or greater good. The person doesn't operate with a "we are one" understanding, which means he/she seeks to gain through manipulation by authenticity rather than non-authenticity. Anything gained through non-authenticity only leads to narrow victories, ongoing trouble, emptiness or fear and unworthiness. This creates an even bigger sense of unworthiness. Again, unworthiness is a fear of not being worthy of others' love and acceptance.

Manipulative folks do not learn, evolve or realize the power of authenticity. Lack of realization of the real power of authenticity and worthiness comes from knowing that one is cherished and accepted for what they really are. In essence, a feeling of unworthiness is often at the core of manipulation.

They Don't Want to Pay the Price Attached to Reach Their Goals

People often manipulate to serve their needs because they do not want to pay the price attached to their goal. They often strive to accomplish the objective or serve their purpose without wanting to give back or pay the price in return.

For instance, if you don't want your partner to leave you, the relationship will take work. You'll have to give your partner love, compassion, understanding, time, loyalty, encouragement, inspiration, a secure future and much more.

A manipulator may not want his/her partner to leave them, but they don't want to pay the price of maintaining a happy, secure and healthy relationship, whereby the partner will never leave them. They may not want to be loyal or spend much time with their partner, and yet they expect them to stay. When people are not ready to pay the price of accomplishing what they want, they may resort to manipulation or underhanded techniques to achieve these goals without paying the price attached to them.

Similarly, if a manipulative person wants to be promoted in his/her workplace, rather than working hard, staying past work hours, upgrading their skills or getting a degree, they will simply manipulate their way into the position. The person is not prepared to pay the price or do what it takes to be promoted.

At times, it's deeply ingrained in a person's psyche that wants are bad or that he/she shouldn't have any desires since it makes them come across as selfish. Manipulation then becomes a way to get what they desire or need without even asking for it.

Manipulators realize there is a price attached to everything. A person won't do them a favor without expecting a favor in return. They won't keep getting things if they don't demonstrate kindness and gratitude. A person won't love them or have sex with them without getting commitment, loyalty and love in return. Manipulators try to push their luck by trying to get something without paying the price attached to it. It is often the easy way out.

They Think They Won't Get Caught

Another reason people manipulate is because they think they can get away with their sneaky acts and that the victims won't realize they are being manipulated. They are also confident that the victim can't do anything even if their manipulation cover is blown.

What gives manipulators the feeling that they won't be caught? Some people come across as inherently clueless, vulnerable, insecure and naïve. These are the type of people manipulators prey on. They believe a person who has low confidence, a low sense of self-worth or is clueless about the ways of the world is less likely to figure out that he/she is being manipulated.

Also, manipulators know that in the event that their manipulation cover is blown, the victim will not be able to do much. They cleverly pick targets who are low in confidence, self-acceptance, body image or sense of self-worth. It is easier to play on the vulnerabilities of these people than on assertive and self-assured people who won't allow people to take advantage of them.

For example, say a person has low awareness of social dynamics, doesn't understand jokes easily, doesn't identify a prank early, is unable to differentiate between genuine courtesy and sexual advances, can't tell when someone is genuinely attracted to them or simply wants to go to bed with them and other similar social and interpersonal dynamics. That person is more likely to be manipulated.

Manipulators are well aware that their victims can't do anything if they don't even realize that their weaknesses are being misused. They often cash in on the cluelessness of their victims by saying they are imagining things or making something up. An already clueless and unsure person is less likely to question this idea. When you are already reeling under feelings of insecurity, cluelessness and vulnerability, how difficult is it for a manipulator to take advantage of these feelings by reinforcing them further?

Manipulators

Manipulators manipulate because they think they can hurt or upset their victims more than the victims can hurt or upset them. They will almost always target people who come across as nice and vulnerable. When people are oblivious to the dishonesty existing within social relationships, they aren't really accustomed to dishonest allegiances. This doesn't equip them with the means to confront or counter dishonesty, which makes them less aware of being manipulated.

They Aren't Able to Accept Their Shortcomings

When people are unable to come to terms with their shortcomings or do not accept the responsibility or accountability for their faults, there is an inherent need to make others feel lesser than them.

If manipulators aren't good enough or feel miserable about themselves, there is a desire to make others feel equally worthless or miserable about themselves. When a person believes he/she is unworthy of someone, they will manipulate the person to feel unworthy, too. They can then gain control over his/her perception that they need the manipulator in their life to feel worthy. By putting others down or gaining control over others, they experience a form of pseudo superiority. If they can't be good enough for others, they make others feel like they aren't good enough to retain control over them.

In effect, manipulators don't want their victims to realize that they (the manipulators) aren't good enough or unworthy of them (the victims). The manipulator will therefore carefully cultivate a feeling of helplessness and unworthiness within the victim to keep them hooked to him/her. If a person realizes that he/she is more attractive, intelligent, richer, capable, efficient, self-sufficient etc., the higher their chances will be of leaving the manipulator. On the other hand, if the manipulator injects a feeling of the person not being 'complete,' they'll need someone to 'complete' them.

Manipulators are not able to accept their shortcomings or deal with criticism. They are often grappling with deep psychological issues or insecurities. By manipulating others, they do not have to confront their own insecurities to feel higher than others. For someone operating with such a narrow perspective, even a little correction, feedback or criticism can seem like a huge defeat.

People who manipulate don't know how to deal with defeat. When you hesitate to give feedback because the person will get defensive or blow things out of proportion or won't take things in the right spirit, it may be a sign you are dealing with someone who can't come to terms with criticism.

Notice how manipulators will seldom express feelings of gratitude or thankfulness. They find it challenging to be grateful to others because, in their view, by doing so they are increasing their sense of being obligated to another person, which doesn't give them an upper hand in any relationship.

For example, if you do someone a huge favor, they feel obliged to return that favor, which puts you above them in the relationship dynamics until they return the favor. Manipulators don't want to give you the upper hand by feeling obliged to you. Therefore, they will demonstrate minimal gratefulness, so you don't believe you've done something huge for them or that they are obliged to you. The idea is to always be one-up on you, and this feeling of being indebted to you doesn't make them feel one-up.

Chapter 4: Manipulation and Neuro Linguistic Programming

What is Neuro Linguistic Programming?

Neuro Linguistic Programming, or NLP, in simplest terms is the programming language of your mind. We've all had instances where we attempted to communicate with someone who doesn't speak our language. The outcome? They didn't understand us!

You go to a restaurant abroad and ask for a fancy steak but end up receiving insipid stew owing to the misinterpretation of language and codes.

This is precisely what happens when we try to communicate with our subconscious mind. We think we are commanding it to give us happier relationships, more money, a better job and other, similar things. However, if that's not what is actually showing up, something is being lost in translation. The subconscious/unconscious mind has the power to help us accomplish our goals only if we program it using codes it recognizes and understands.

If you are asking your unconscious mind for steak and receiving stew, it is time to speak its language. Think of NLP as a user manual for the brain. When people master NLP, they become fluent in the language of the subconscious mind, which is excellent when it comes to re-programming their own and other people's thoughts, ideas and beliefs. This gives them the power to influence and persuade people, and on the downside, even manipulate them.

Neuro Linguistic Programming is a set of techniques, methods and tools for enhancing communication with deeper layers of our brain. It is an approach that combines personal development, psychotherapy and communication. Its creators (John Grinder and Richard Bandler) claim that there is a strong link between language, behavior patterns and neurological processes, which can be used for enhancing learning and personal development.

Influence versus Manipulation

So, do you believe a hammer is a tool of utility or destruction? Well, it depends on how you use it, right? Or what purpose you use it for.

NLP is potent when it comes to getting people to do what you want them to. It is the hammer that can be used to fix a nail in the wall or destroy a piece of wood. Similarly, NLP can be used to build something positive, or it can be used for a destructive purpose (manipulation).

NLP and manipulation have nearly the same meaning. Both are about generating the desired effect on other people without obvious exertion.

However, one key difference between influence and manipulation is that the latter is meant to influence others to meet the manipulator's selfish goals through means that can be unfair, unlawful, sneaky, or insidious. Things are contrived through underhanded methods to turn out in favor of the manipulator. A manipulator often preys on the insecurities, fears and guilt of other people. In turn, victims of manipulation feed dissatisfied, frustrated, trapped and unhappy.

Conversely, influence is the ability to inspire people in an admirable, charismatic and honorable way. We are often inspired by influential people and aspire to model our life on theirs. There is a general feeling of positivity related to them, and we feel positively impacted in their company. Not every influence is positive, which is why we use terms such as "bad influence" to signify a person's negative effect on us. However, manipulation is never categorized as good or bad. It always operates with sinister motives. That is the primary difference between influence and manipulation.

Influence is a double-edged sword that can be used positively and negatively, while manipulation only operates with a negative, narrow and selfish perspective to meet the objectives of the manipulator.

While manipulation has self-centered and questionable motives, influence can also be positive. In contrast to manipulation, influence has positive connotations, which considers other people's needs, goals and desires. Don't we, as parents, want to influence our children to lead happier and healthier lives? Similarly, as a manager, we want to influence our team to put in their best efforts.

Just like the hammer discussed above, people can use NLP for positively or negatively influencing people to meet their own selfish objectives (manipulation). NLP is a mind control tool that can do both – build and damage.

How is NLP Used for Manipulating People?

NLP training is conducted in a pyramid-like structure, with sophisticated techniques reserved for high-end seminars. It is a complex subject (whoever said anything related to the human mind would be easy?). However, to simplify a complicated concept, NLPers, or people who practice NLP, pay keen attention to people they work with. They watch everything from eye movements to skin flushes to pupil dilation in order to determine what type of information people are processing.

Through observation, NLPers can tell which side of the brain is dominant in a person. Similarly, they can tell what sense is the most active within the person's brain. The eye movements can determine how their brain stores and uses information. It is also easy to decipher whether the person is stating facts (telling the truth) or making up facts (lying) by looking at his/her eye movements.

After gathering this invaluable information, NLP manipulators will subtly mirror and mimic their victims (including speech, body language, mannerisms, verbal linguistic patterns and more) to give a feeling of being 'one among them.'

NLPers will fake social clues to lead their victims into dropping their guard and entering a more open, receptive and suggestible state of mind, where they become ready to absorb whatever information their mind is fed. Manipulators will cleverly use language that focuses on a person's predominant senses.

For example, if a person is focused on his/her visual sense, the NLP manipulator will most likely use it to his/her advantage optimally by saying something like, "Do you see where I am coming from?" "Can you see what I am trying to tell you?" or "See it this way?" Similarly, if a person is a predominantly auditory person, the manipulator will speak to them using auditory metaphors like, "Just hear me out once, Tim" or "I hear you."

By mirroring their victim's body language and verbal linguistic patterns, NLP experts, or NLPer manipulators, attempt to accomplish a clear objective – building rapport. As discussed earlier, manipulators also try to accomplish this by sharing too much too soon or building early intimacy. The objective is the same – to strike a rapport with their victims, which then makes it easy for the victims to let down their guard.

Once the manipulator uses NLP to build rapport and get the victim to let down his guard through clever use of body language and verbal patterns, the victim becomes more open and suggestible. Fake social cues are fed to the victim to make their minds more malleable.

Once they build a rapport, NLPers will begin to lead the victim into increased interaction in a sublime manner. After having mirrored the victim and establishing in the victim's subconscious mind that he/she (the manipulator) is one among them (the victim), the manipulator increases his/her chances of getting the victim to do whatever the manipulator wants. They will subtly change their behavior and language to influence their victim's actions.

The techniques can include leading questions, sublime language patterns and a host of other NLP techniques to maneuver the person's mind wherever they want. The victim, on the other hand, often doesn't realize what is happening. In their view, everything is occurring naturally/organically or according to their consent.

Of course, manipulators (however skilled) may not be able to use NLP to get people to behave in a manner that is completely out of character. However, it can be used to steer people's responses in the desired direction. For instance, you can't convince a fundamentally ethical and truthful person to act in a dishonest manner. However, you can use it to get a person to think in a specific direction or line of thought. Manipulators use NLP to engineer specific responses from a person.

NLP attempts accomplish two ends, eliciting and anchoring. Eliciting occurs when NLPers use language and leading to draw their victims into an emotional state. Once the desired state is accomplished, the NLPer will then anchor the emotion with a specific physical clue - for example, tapping on their shoulder. This simply means that an NLPer can invoke the same emotion in you by tapping your shoulder.

For example, let us say the NLP manipulator makes you feel depressed or unworthy using language, leading and other NLP techniques. This is followed by tapping the back of your hands in a specific manner to create anchoring. Thus, each time they want to create an emotion of being disillusioned, depressed and unworthy in you, they will tap the back of your palm. It is nothing but conditioning you to feel in a certain way with linked physical clues.

Now that you have a fair idea of what NLP is or how manipulators can use it for submission, what can you do to guard yourself against NLP manipulators?

Here are some tips to prevent NLPers from pulling their remarkably smart yet sneaky tricks on you:

1. Be wary of people mirroring your body language. Agreed, you didn't know this until now, but people imitating or copying your body language is one of the biggest red flags of them trying to manipulate, influence or persuade you to act in a desired manner. I really enjoy testing these NLP experts using subtle hand gestures and leg movements to gauge if they are indeed mirroring my body language to establish a rapport.

If they follow suit, that's my clue to flee! Experienced NLPers have mastered the art of subtle mirroring, which means you may not even realize they are imitating your actions. NLP beginners will instantly imitate the exact same movement in their eagerness to establish a feeling of oneness. Good way for you to call their bluff!

2. Confuse with eye movements. Another fantastic way to call an NLP manipulator's bluff is to notice if they are paying very close attention to your eyes or eye movements. NLP users often examine their target or victim's very carefully. The eye movements are scrutinized to gauge how you access and store information.

In effect, they want to determine what parts of the brain you are utilizing to gather clues about your thoughts and feelings. I say beat this by darting your eyes all around the place randomly. Move them upwards and downwards or from side to side in no clear pattern. You are throwing your NLP manipulator off course. Make it appear natural. Their calibration will go down the wayside.

3. Beware of people's touch. As we discussed earlier, one of the techniques NLPers use is anchoring. If you know a person practices NLP, and you are in an especially heightened or intense emotional condition, do not allow them to touch you in any manner. Just throw them off course by suddenly laughing hard or flying into a fit of rage. Basically, you are confusing them about the emotion they need to anchor. Even if they attempt to establish a physical clue to invoke certain emotions, they'll be left with a mixed bag of crazy laughter, rage and whatever else you did.

4. Watch out for permissive language. Typical language used by NLPers includes "be relaxed," "relax and enjoy this," and other similar statements. Beware of this NLP, hypnotist style language that induces you into a state of deep relaxation or trance to get you to think or act in a specific manner. Skilled or covert manipulators rarely command in a straightforward manner.

They will cleverly seek your permission to give you the impression that you are doing what they want you to do out of your own free will (one of their many sinister tricks). If you observe experienced hypnotists, they will never outright command you to do anything but seek your permission to make it appear as if it is being done organically, with your consent.

5. Guard Against Gibberish. Watch out for mumbo jumbo that just doesn't make any logical sense or twisted/complicated statements that mean little.

For example, "As you free the feeling of being held by your thoughts, you will find yourself in alignment with the voice of your success." Does this make any sense? NLP manipulators won't say anything purposeful, but rather, they will program your emotional state to lead it where they want to.

One of the best ways to guard against this sort of hypnotism-NLP induced manipulation is to urge the manipulator to be more specific. "Can you be clearer about this?" "Can you specify exactly what you mean by that?" It won't just interrupt their cleverly set technique but will also force the interaction into precise language, thus breaking the trance brought about through ambiguous words and phrases.

6. Don't quickly agree to anything. If you find yourself being compelled to make an instant decision about something important, and it feels like you are steered in a specific direction, escape the situation. Wait a day to make a decision. Do not be swept or led into making a decision that you do not want to make on an impulse. Sales professionals are adept at manipulating buyers into purchasing something they don't need using sneaky manipulation and NLP tactics. When someone rushes you into a decision, it should be a warning signal to back off and hold on until you've thought more about the situation.

Chapter 5: Techniques for Outsmarting Manipulators

Like it or wince, the world is full of wolves in sheep's clothing. You can't do much about pathological and emotional manipulators who are out to leverage your feelings and emotions to satisfy their wants. However, you can beat them in their own game by using a bunch of outsmarting techniques. Manipulation, if not recognized and handled efficiently, can tear down your sense of self-worth and sanity. By recognizing and coping with manipulation, you are standing up for yourself and not allowing sinister manipulators to fulfill their agenda by tramping on your feelings.

Here are some smart and effective hacks for outsmarting manipulators in their own game:

1. Put the spotlight on them by posing probing queries. Manipulators are constantly demanding things or making offers to their victims. As a victim, you will be made to feel that you need to prove yourself all the time. You'll often go out of the way to fulfill these demands. Stop. Each time you find them coming up with an unreasonable request, shoot back a few probing questions and shift the focus on them.

For example, Does this seem like a legitimate and reasonable request to you?

Do you think what you've asked from me is fair or ethical?

Do I have the right to refuse?

Are you requesting or demanding that I do this?

What do I gain from doing this?

Are you really expecting that I will do this?

Are you reasonably justified in expecting me to do this?

Who stands to gain the most from this?

Basically, you ask questions that show them the mirror, where they can witness their real, sinister ploy. If the manipulator is self-aware or realizes that you've seen through their motives, they will most likely withdraw the request.

Manipulators try to put the focus on you as if you are unworthy or 'bad' if you don't do something for them. You've got to put the focus back on them by making them think whether their request is indeed justified or reasonable, thus, making them come across as people with evil motives.

Questions will eventually force the manipulator to realize that you are seeing through their game. The focus of the action will now shift from you to them.

For example, if you refuse the manipulator's request, the onus of justifying your action isn't on you. By asking probing questions, you are asking the manipulator to justify the reasonability of their request. So, instead of feeling guilty about refusing something, you are making the manipulator realize that he/she is at fault for having unreasonable expectations.

Also, let your manipulator know that you don't accept being treated the way they treat you. Make it sufficiently clear that you don't appreciate their ways.

For instance, if you are already preoccupied with something, and the manipulator makes a request to do something for them, say something to the effect that, "I do not appreciate it when I am already working on something and you make another request of me before I finish the current task."

Similarly, when a person is trying to force you into making a decision that benefits them, say something like, "I am able to make my own decisions and would really appreciate if you don't coerce me into making a decision in a hurry." You are being assertive and telling off your manipulator without being rude. You are simply standing up for your right and informing them that you have the right to take your time to decide, and it could backfire if they pressure you into making a decision.

2. Take your time in fulfilling a request. Not only will manipulators make unreasonable requests, they will also pressure you into making a quick

decision. They want to wield optimal control, influence and pressure over you to get you to act in a specific way immediately. Manipulators realize that if you take more time, things may not go in their favor.

Do the exact opposite of what they want by taking more time. Sales people are always focused on closing the deal soon. Distance yourself from the manipulator's persuasion and take time to arrive at a decision. You don't have to act right away, however much the person tries to pressure you.

Take control over the person and situation by saying something like, "I'd like more time to think about it" or "It is my right to take more time to think about a decision as important as this" or "I need to evaluate the pros and cons before I arrive at a decision."

You can use this time to negotiate in your favor.

3. Say no assertively yet diplomatically. This is an art which will only come with practice. You don't want to offend the manipulator by saying a straight no. Yet, you want to be firm and let them know you won't allow them to walk all over you. Stand your ground, while still being polite and courteous. You don't have to feel guilty about your right to refuse an unreasonable request.

If you aren't up for something, say, "I understand you want me to do this, but I also feel I am not up for it right now." Another way to articulate your needs is, "The best thing for me to do right now is…"

One of the best comebacks is to focus on your needs over those of the manipulator without guilt.

One of the sneakiest tricks used by manipulators is to make you feel guilty every time you don't comply with their request. When you stop feeling guilty about standing up for yourself or exercising your right to be treated with respect, manipulators become powerless.

4. Know your fundamental rights and worth. The most important weapon when you are dealing with manipulators is to know when your rights are being violated. You have the absolute right to stand up for those rights and defend yourself. You have the fundamental right to be treated with respect and honor.

Again, you have the right to express your emotions, needs and feelings. You have the right to establish your priorities, refuse something without feeling guilty, the right to protect yourself/love ones from harm, the right to acquire what you pay for, and the right to live a happy, healthy and fulfilling life.

These are your boundaries, and you can remind people to respect these rights. Psychological manipulators often want to take away your fundamental rights in a bid to exercise greater control over you. However, the power and authority to take charge of your life lies with you, and you shouldn't miss an opportunity to remind your manipulator that you alone are in control of your life. Distance yourself from people who do not respect these basic boundaries.

5. Maintain your distance. One of the most effective ways to spot a manipulator is by observing how they act differently with different folks or in diverse situations. Of course, we all come with some amount of social differential, but if the person is habitually behaving out of character in extremes, he/she may be a master manipulator.

Think, being unnaturally polite to one person and the next minute downright rude to another or acting vulnerable one moment and then becoming aggressive within the next. When you witness this type of behavior, maintain your distance from the person. Avoid interacting with these people until absolutely necessary. Otherwise, you may end up inviting trouble. There are plenty of reasons people manipulate, and it is very psychologically complex. Don't attempt to fix manipulators all the time. It isn't your duty to change them. Just save yourself by moving on.

6. Avoid blaming yourself, or personalization. One of the smoothest tricks used by manipulators is to make their victims feel like it is always their (the victim's) fault. Irrespective of what the manipulator does or knows, they will never take accountability for their faults. They will always blame the victim for all their wrongs.

As a victim of manipulation, you need to stop personalizing. The problem is not with you since you are simply being made to feel that it's your fault, so you give away your rights to the manipulator and become powerless.

Do not be led into thinking that you are the problem, or the problem lies with you. I knew a friend who was constantly chided by her husband for working hard to support the family. He never missed an opportunity to remind her that she wasn't a good wife or mother because she was always working. In her mind, she was working hard to give her children a great future (which really didn't make her a bad mother).

However, in his attempt to gain absolute control over her, he constantly blamed her and made her feel incompetent as a wife and mother. Initially, my friend believed everything that was told to her about being a bad mother and wife. However, over a period of time, she realized she was simply being blamed because her husband couldn't come to terms with his own shortcomings.

Ask yourself these questions before blaming yourself:

Are you being treated with respect?

Are the person's demands reasonable?

Do I feel good about myself while interacting with this person?

These are important clues about the real problem.

7. Set consequences for manipulative behavior. Psychological and pathological manipulators will always insist on disregarding your rights. They rarely take no for an answer, often flying into a rage or becoming aggressive. Recognize and state consequences clearly if they resort to aggression as a response to your refusal to comply with their unreasonable request.

An effectively communicated and asserted consequence can be used to pin down a manipulative person and compel him/her to change their stand from violating your rights to respecting them. By reinforcing consequences, you are uncovering their hidden agendas and making them bring about a shift in their attitude towards you. Basically, you are cutting off their power.

It is important to stand up against the manipulator's bullying tactics. They will often try to scare you into giving in to their demands. Manipulators claim to hold on to your weaknesses to feel superior and powerful. If you stay passive and play along, they'll take greater advantage of you. Confront them and exercise your rights. Since manipulators are inherently cowardly, they'll retreat.

Research has proven that being manipulative is closely linked to an abusive childhood or being victims of bullying. This in no way justifies the act of a bully. However, when you keep this in mind, you'll find healthier and more effective ways to respond to the manipulator.

8. Value yourself for who you are. Manipulators feed on the low self-esteem of their victims. They'll always catch people who are vulnerable, unsure, low on confidence and don't know their real worth.

Rarely will the manipulator go after people with a high self-esteem or sense of self-worth. If you can stay strong and take the manipulator head on by establishing your self-worth, it is evident you won't allow anyone to control you.

9. Silence is golden. Manipulators love drama. They will often provoke feelings of anger, fear, sadness and more in you to think they've scored points over you. The best way to deal with this is to stay calm and practice deep breathing. Concentrate on your breath and how the body feels. Try to relax your muscles and look the manipulator in the eye.

This simple body language of confidence and assertion can throw them off the tangent. A manipulator doesn't know how to deal with your calmness in such a situation. They are fully equipped to deal with your anger and fear. However, they don't expect you to react with calmness. It infuriates them and tells them the ploy doesn't seem to be effective on you. They will learn that your emotions remain unchanged and shift to another target.

Don't get me wrong here. I am certainly not advocating giving up on a relationship at the first sign of manipulation. Manipulation can slowly pop up even in otherwise happy and fulfilling relationships, and it doesn't necessarily signify the end of a relationship. Before taking any drastic step, have a frank and open conversation with your partner or the person who is manipulating you. Gather the courage to ask them why they are doing this to you. These answers may give you vital clues into their state of mind and your next move.

If you've already attempted to have an open communication with your partner and they wouldn't have any of it, it may be time to explore other options such as therapy or counseling. However, you both have to be committed to the pursuit of overcoming manipulation within the relationship.

10. Practice self-care. Coping with a manipulative relationship can be intensely exhausting and stressful. Ensure you practice self-care to nurture your mind, body and spirit, and don't let the manipulation take its toll on you. It is common to feel stressed at the end of each interaction with a manipulator (been there, done that).

When you feel your mental energy drained after communication with a manipulator, do meditation, yoga or deep breathing. It infuses a sense of calm into your being. Do something enjoyable and exciting to prevent the negative feelings from spoiling your day. Go for a long walk in the midst of nature or talk to someone you trust.

Chapter 6: Dealing with Manipulation in Relationships

Emotional manipulation or being in a manipulative relationship is one of the most unfortunate things a person can experience. Not only does it destroy your sense of self-worth, but it also prevents you from enjoying fulfilling and rewarding relationships in the future. Manipulation goes against the ethos of a healthy, happy, positive and inspiring relationship.

While we are all in some way or another manipulating our loved ones, it becomes sinister when it hits at a person's emotions or sense of self-worth for fulfilling a selfish agenda. Here are some effective deals for dealing with manipulation in relationships:

1. Closely observe your feelings after every interaction. Do a majority of your conversations or interactions with your partner make you feel confused, unworthy or overcome by self-doubt? By doing a routine check of your feelings, you will be able to identify a clear cause.

For example, if you realize that you always feel guilty after a conversation with your partner, rewind to the conversation and go over what your partner said after each interaction. How did it start?

What are the typical words and phrases they use while talking to you? Is there a pattern to what they say and how they make you feel?

It would be even better if you can make a note of your feelings to easily identify the emerging pattern.

Tell yourself that the problem is them and not you. Remember that you are only being hoodwinked into thinking it is your fault or you aren't good enough. The manipulator is most likely dealing with grave issues of their own, which they are incapable of handling effectively. This is only to help you establish a context for their acts, not to make you feel sympathetic towards them. Keep in mind, manipulators seldom deserve sympathy!

2. Assess your relationship objectively. If you can't determine if you are truly in a manipulative relationship, get a reality check by talking to friends or people you trust.

Ask them for an objective assessment of your relationship frankly. Do they think your partner has unreasonable expectations of you? Do they think your partner is taking advantage of you? Do they think you are being emotionally vulnerable?

Sometimes, by talking to a third person, we gain a perspective we hadn't considered before. It'll probably give you a new way of looking at things, which will allow you to act immediately if you are being manipulated.

3. Confront the manipulator. Consider various angles before approaching and confronting your manipulator. They most likely won't admit to their manipulative acts, especially if you sound unsure and nervous.

Rather than making statements about how they have been "using you" or "taking advantage of you," get down to specifics. How does a specific action or certain words make you feel? List specific instances where you felt you were taken advantage of. Follow this up with a positive and gentle, yet assertive, request to mend their behavior.

You are communicating to the manipulator that you are aware of their tricks, which makes them more cautious while manipulating you. In the same vein, you are also giving them an opportunity to get their act together. It will take real effort and commitment on your part to move out of an emotionally manipulative relationship. You will have to stay vigilant and develop limitless reserves of self-esteem and positivity.

4. Hit hard at the center of their gravity. If nothing else seems to work, hit the manipulator hard at his/her center of gravity. They'll often resort to evil strategies such as befriending your friends and then speaking evil about you or tempting you with a reward and then backing off or not honoring their commitment.

Since you know the person inside out, hit them where it hurts the most. Their center may be their friends, followers or anything they think is integral to their existence. Use this knowledge to beat them at their own game.

5. Don't fit in with their ideas. The key to avoid being manipulated is to reinvent yourself and have your own ideas about things rather than subscribing to theirs. Manipulators will shove their ideas down your throat since they need to control you to further their agenda. Have your own clear views, ideas and opinions about various aspects of your life. Consistently drilling a particular idea into your mind is how they are able to successfully confine you in a box.

Don't try to fit in, focus on reinvention. Work hard towards standing out from the rest. Be different, unique and remarkable in your own way. Personal growth and building your self-esteem is the key for fighting manipulation.

6. Don't compromise. Guilt is a powerful emotion leveraged by manipulators. They will use your self-doubt and guilt to their advantage. The agenda is to tip your sense of balance and instill a sense of uncertainty within you. This uncertainty eventually drives you to compromise on your values, ideals and goals.

Avoid feeling guilty or compromising. Don't doubt yourself or your abilities. Even though you are in a relationship with a person, you don't owe them anything if you are not treated with respect. Every person deserves to feel wonderful and positive about themselves. If a person doesn't make you feel good about yourself or your accomplishments, there may be a problem. Have a firm belief in your values and ideals. Don't compromise on your values, beliefs, goals and ideals. Remember, you deserve to feel great about yourself and your achievements. There should be a strong sense of self-belief, self-assuredness and confidence in what you are doing.

A manipulator becomes powerless in the face of high self-confidence. They start losing their influence once you learn to operate with confidence and refuse to compromise on anything that undermines your self-respect or core values.

7. Don't seek permission. This is like handing the manipulator the pass to manipulate you as they wish. The trouble is, since childhood, we've been conditioned to seek permission. As an infant, we seek permission to eat and sleep. All through school we are seeking permission to visit the bathroom, eat our lunch or drink water.

A direct consequence of this is, even as grown-ups, we don't stop seeking permission from people close to us. Instead of informing your partner you are planning to meet a friend over lunch, you'll subconsciously ask them if it is alright if you plan something with your friend. By constantly and habitually seeking permission, you are only giving the control of your life to someone else, especially if he/she is a more manipulative type.

Don't be overly concerned about being polite or making others feel good at the cost of your own comfort and happiness. Remember, you have the right to live your life exactly the way you want to. Emotional manipulation is about making you feel beholden or enslaved by some imaginary rule that exists only in the mind of the manipulator. They'll never want you to feel self-sufficient and make your own decisions because that diminishes their hold over you.

There's no need to bow to their authoritative dictates or consult them before everything you do, unless it does impact them in an important manner. I happened to have a co-worker who would seek his girlfriend's permission even before going for a coffee break or out for lunch. It was ridiculous the way she treated him and tried to control every move of his. Predictably, the relationship ended on a sour note.

However, no one can make you feel miserable without your permission. And by constantly seeking permission, you are giving your partner the permission to make you feel miserable – if that makes sense. You can disregard the manipulator's obsession with confining you anytime by living your life the way you want to, without their interference or permission.

8. Be open to new opportunities. The manipulator wants you to put all your eggs in their basket, so they can throw away the basket whenever they fancy. Don't lock yourself into them or be tied

down by a commitment you aren't comfortable making. Don't be content or accept your current life. If you are in a highly manipulative or emotionally/physically abusive relationship, attempt to break free and explore other relationships or opportunities.

Manipulators in relationships often take advantage of the fact that their partner is "used to them," "addicted to them," "can't do without them," or "can't get anyone better." We often stay in abusive relationships because we believe that we don't deserve any better or won't get anyone better. There is a fear of loneliness or a false sense of being in the cocoon of a relationship.

Break free from such self-limiting and unhealthy thought patterns. Of course, you deserve better in life or will find someone who treats you with respect and dignity. To keep you in your place, manipulators will resort to plenty of name calling. If you express a desire, they will make you feel like you are arrogant, selfish, proud, cold, and inhumane and many other uncharitable labels.

They want to keep you dependent on them. By seeking out new opportunities for jobs, relationships, hobbies etc., you are only weakening their control over you. Seek out new people, make new friends, join a hobby club, volunteer with a non-governmental organization. Do something purposeful and meaningful that gives you the opportunity to meet new people and live a more intentional life. This is the only way to start becoming self-sufficient and independent.

9. Don't be a baby. If you are fooled once or twice, you are vulnerable, but if you constantly let people walk all over you without learning your lessons, you are a downright idiot. Stop letting manipulators take advantage of your gullibility. Develop self-awareness about manipulators and know how they operate. Have enough self-respect to refuse manipulators.

I know a lot of people who sleep walk through life, allow people to take advantage of them and then blame others for their situation. You can't go around oblivious to manipulators who are trying to use you to fulfill their agenda. Rather than blaming the evil around you, become smart and take control of your life. Yes, the unfortunate truth about life is that negative and manipulative people exist. They take advantage of people to further their agenda.

However, this shouldn't be your ticket to making the same mistakes again and again and crying foul. Manipulators cannot manipulate without the permission of their victims. Accept responsibility for your success and failure. If you are outsmarted or out strategized, it isn't someone else's fault. Learn from past mistakes. Watch out for a pattern that may reveal your own vulnerabilities. Don't keep trusting the wrong people again and again.

Similarly, don't keep giving a chronically manipulative person multiple chances. Break free from them. Remove manipulators from your life. Commit to the pursuit of surrounding yourself with positive, encouraging and like-minded folks who don't take advantage of you.

Remember, you have complete control over your life. Place your bets on yourself and not on other people. If you place your bets on other people or rely excessively on other people for your happiness, you make yourself more vulnerable to manipulation.

Again, manipulation victims are not very confident about their judgments. Learn to trust your judgments and instincts. You know what is good for you much better than anyone else. Don't go around asking people things such as, "What am I good at?" "Who is the real me?" etc. You are simply opening the doors of manipulation. Don't go around demonstrating your lack of understanding about yourself.

Again, I know a lot of people who go around seeking constant validation from others. They look at other people to define them. These people won't even buy a pair of trousers if it isn't approved by others. Why should others define you?

Define yourself and trust your judgment. Winners are not people who have a more evolved ability to listen to others. They are the ones who have developed the ability to tune in to their beliefs and judgments. They don't rely on external validation or approval of their beliefs. An established trust in your beliefs and judgments makes manipulators powerless. When you don't seek validation from others, they don't have an upper hand in how they make you think and feel. Start trusting your instinct and judgment!

10. Dependent manipulators. This is a little opposed to the stereotypical image of a manipulator, but they exist. Contrary to most manipulators, a dependent manipulator will constantly make you feel like they are powerless and completely dependent on you. They accord you the higher position in a relationship to such an extent that you feel emotionally exhausted while dealing with them.

The way to handle this type of manipulation is to gradually get them to make decisions. Make them realize that they are as much responsible for their well-being as you are. Consciously put them into positions where they are forced to make a decision. Talk to them about how their lack of responsibility to decision making is stressful for you. Over time, they may enjoy taking responsibility.

Chapter 7: Solid Tips for Increasing Your Self-Esteem

The core of being manipulated is experiencing feelings of incompetency and unworthiness. Rarely will you see confident people with high self-esteem and a high sense of self-worth being manipulated. Psychological manipulators thrive on making people feel unworthy and imbalanced. By inducing this feeling of insufficiency in their victims, they attempt to gain greater power and control over the victims and, in turn, use their sense of powerlessness to fulfill selfish agendas.

One of the best ways to immunize yourself from manipulation is to develop high self-esteem and self-confidence. By having a high sense of self-worth and a positive opinion about yourself, you are preventing hungry manipulators from sabotaging you.

Here are some powerful tips for increasing your overall self-esteem to make you less susceptible to manipulation:

1. Hold your inner critic. Yes, we all have that niggling inner frenemy who doesn't fail to remind us of how incapable we are at doing something or how miserable our life is compared to others. This inner voice shapes your thoughts and opinions about yourself.

Minimize your negative voice and consciously replace it with more positive and constructive terms. For instance, "I am so bad at this" can be replaced with, "I may not be good at this, but that shouldn't stop me from learning everything I can about it and mastering it." You've just given a positive twist to a hopeless statement. Choose to use more hopeful, positive and inspiring words while speaking to yourself.

Stay, "Stop," loudly when you find your inner critic rearing its monstrous head. You can also resort to a physical gesture like pinching yourself slowly or biting your lips each time you find your inner critic in hyper active mode.

2. Be more compassionate towards other people and treat them well. One of the best ways to raise your own self-esteem is to treat other people with greater compassion. When you make others feel good about themselves, you automatically feel great about yourself. When you treat people well, you inspire them to treat you well in return.

Practice kindness in your daily life by volunteering for a social cause (a huge self-esteem booster), hold the door for people, listen to someone vent, let people pass through your lane while driving, buy coffee or treats for random people, encourage a person who is feeling deflated and similar other gestures. These will go a long way in building your self-esteem.

3. Try new things. People who are constantly trying new things or reinventing themselves are almost always high on self-esteem. They are constantly challenging themselves by stepping outside their comfort zones. They try their hand at everything and appreciate various experiences, which increase feelings of competency.

When you keep learning new things and developing your skills, you feel wonderful about yourself. You avoid falling into a rut. Keep trying a new adventure or picking up a new skill periodically. Nudge yourself to be active, passionate and productive. Set your spirit and soul into motion every now and then by taking up a hobby, picking up a new skill or reading an inspiring book.

4. Avoid comparisons. You are slowly destroying yourself by constantly comparing yourself or your life to others. There is no victory in this; you'll always lose! It is a trap that will only make you feel more inadequate and unworthy.

Instead, look at where you were a few years ago and how far you've come to accomplish where you are today. Focus on your accomplishments and achievements today compared to a few years ago.

Albert Einstein famously said, "Everybody is a genius. But if you judge a fish by its ability to climb a tree, it will spend its whole life believing that it is stupid." Don't be that fish!

5. Spend time with positive people. Another great way to build your self-esteem is to surround yourself with people who support, encourage and inspire you. They should be people you look up to and should be able to influence you positively. It can be anyone from a professor to a mentor to a manager to a good friend.

Avoid interacting with people who focus on your flaws or try to bring you down at every available opportunity to feel superior about themselves. Look out for dream snatchers or people who laugh at your dreams or your ability to accomplish your goals. Self-esteem thrives in a positive environment in the midst of positive people. Be with people who make you feel good about yourself.

Also, be mindful of the books, websites and social media pages that you read. Let them charge your energy, not sap it. Don't read magazines that peddle unrealistic body images. Listen to podcasts that are naturally uplifting, empowering and inspiring the next time you find yourself with some free time at hand. Watch television shows that uplift your spirit.

6. Sweat it out. Countless studies have established a high correlation between exercise and a healthy self-esteem. Exercise leads to enhanced mental and physical health, which in turn, reduces stress and makes you feel good. It also brings more discipline into your life, which invariably increases self-esteem.

Exercise doesn't have to be boring. You can take up something fun and interesting like dance, cycling, swimming, aerobics, kickboxing and more. Anything that helps you sweat and gives you a small sense of accomplishment at the end. Physical activity boosts the secretion of endorphins within the brain, which makes us "feel good." And we all know how feeling good can have a positive effect on our self-perception and self-esteem.

7. Practice forgiveness. Is there some grudge that you've been holding for a long time? It may be related to an ex-partner, a family member during your growing up years, a friend who betrayed you or even yourself. Don't hold on to feelings of bitterness. Overcome past feelings of shame, guilt and regret, since holding on to them will only suck you further into the circle of negativity.

Conclusion

Thank you again for getting a copy this book!

I hope it was able to help you to understand not just the ways through which people manipulate you but also powerful ways in which you can immunize yourself against manipulators.

The next step is to simply use all the powerful strategies and techniques used in the book to understand manipulative motives and to prevent people from manipulating you in relationships, at work and within your social circle.

There are plenty of practical tips, wisdom nuggets and real-life illustrations to help you gain a solid understanding of how manipulation works and how it can be fought in your everyday life.

Persuasion

The Complete Psychologist's Guide to Highly Effective Persuasion and Manipulation Techniques – Influence People with NLP, Mind Control and Human Behavior Psychology

Introduction

"The only real power available to the leader is the power of persuasion."
– Lyndon B. Johnson, 36th President of the United States

The ability to connect is an essential trait for daily living. Connecting through communication is a successful way to accomplish what you want throughout your day. Communication is a skill that you need to improve and foster consistently.

A large portion of my day as a psychologist requires me to use a variety of communication skills with clients. Many of the conversations were typical day-to-day connections, but occasionally, it was more high-risk than that. When it is necessary, I found turning to the power of persuasion a powerful tool to persuade someone; to guide them through reasonable argument or discourse. The communication is graceful and delicate. When it is employed correctly, it can deliver immense guidance to others.

Persuasion is an art that intrinsically motivates people to change their behaviors, both in thought and action. This is not a form of manipulation or deception. It is a natural action without force. Having a cheering squad on your side as you strive for success can be achieved through persuasion in both the important and daily conversations. Use this technique to help those around you see what you are aiming for and how they can help you achieve success. Thankfully, persuasion and other communication techniques can be learned and implemented with time and dedication. Become able to influence people in any setting with this one set of skills.

This book is a guide on how to use persuasion to control your own mind and influence others daily. I have used my experience as a psychologist to explain how persuasion has been used in various scenarios that I have encountered, both professionally and personally. The important aspect of persuasion is that influence is easy, but correct influence, or guiding influence, is a talent. If your goal is to get people to actually listen to you, know that this is different than just hearing you; they need to understand you.

Persuasion is a method for getting the outside actions of people to do what you want by "controlling," or adjusting, their inside thoughts.

I share my methods to accomplish this throughout this book. These techniques can be used in any scenario. What may come as a surprise is that you are probably already doing many of the persuasive techniques already. This is especially true if you are a naturally compassionate and extroverted person. If you recognize this in yourself as you read along, congratulations, you are already on the path! Now you need to identify exactly what it is that is working, why it works, and how to get even better. For those of you who do not see yourself in the techniques outlined, do not fear. Once you begin putting some of these into practice, you will find it is a natural method of communicating.

The way we behave as humans is very foreseeable. There are personal and societal habits. The way to succeed in life is to understand these repetitions and master the art of mind control with persuasion and influence.

The following chapters are filled with relevant examples, but more importantly, with directions and advice you can follow, not just theories and contemplation. Consider this your go-to manual on how to truly influence others in any situation.

Section 1 Program Your Mind: Understand Persuasion and How to Use It

"You have power over your mind – not outside events. Realize this, and you will find strength."

Put yourself in the driver's seat. How? Grasp the concepts of influence, persuasion, and motivation. Why? These concepts will help to deliver to you everything you desire in life. Everyone can employ the rules of persuasion, but almost no one knows what the rules are or how to apply them. For this reason, throughout my revelation of the science and "secrets" of persuasion, you will be able to accurately influence others. Grab life by the horns and enjoy what you want out of life by inspiring others to take action, and revel in the influence you have on other people. Gain the confidence in yourself and earn the recognition of other people's understanding of your way of thinking. Enjoy prosperity, captivate, magnetize, and succeed all through the power of persuasion.

Think of yourself as an incredibly strong magnet and envision people being pulled to you as if they are little pieces of metal that must be brought in by your magnetism. This is what your life will be like when you practice persuasion and influence. This can be used in any aspect of your life: wealth, personal, and professional. Social environments will become a natural playground for you. Doors that were previously closed to you magically begin to be open, and previously hidden paths will be revealed, so you can walk confidently in your direction of success. The principles shared in this book are tried and true concepts that have the power to transform your life forever. Numerous studies of human behavior and persuasion have been used as the foundation for the techniques given to you. They are here at your fingertips; all you have to do is grab them.

This resource guides you with the knowledge of traditional methodologies of persuasion and how to put these leading strategies to use to gain the influence you seek. These methods explain how to make people trust you in a way that takes others decades to establish. Intimidation and fear will no longer have a place in your life as you face the unknown. Now, you can face it with conviction, power, and integrity, every day, in each situation that challenges you. Dominate your fortune.

Persuasion has a power that this world needs. It is formidable and serious. Each time you come in contact with another person, there is an attempt to guide one another or to encourage them to follow your way of thinking. It does not matter who the people are that connect with one another. They could have the same beliefs or different, be the same race or different, have the same career or different. None of that matters. Persuasion is pervasive. The goal is to be trusted, followed, and *heard*. Sometimes this goal can be for good reasons, and sometimes it can be for bad reasons. For the purpose of this book, we are assuming you are here to learn how to persuade in order to improve lives and better yourself and those around you. You want your community to achieve greatness. It is time for you to rise up and uplift those around you during your ascent.

Chapter 1.1: Traditional Mental Persuasion

"When I'm getting ready to reason with a man, I spend one-third of my time thinking about myself and what I am going to say -- and two-thirds thinking about him and what he is going to say."

Definition and History

Influence is often used interchangeably with the term "persuasion;" however, persuasion is a form of influence and not the other way around. Behavior, motivators, intentions, beliefs, and attitudes can be touched by persuasion in an attempt to influence one or more of those elements. Professional persuasion is often exerted to alter the thoughts of a group regarding something happening and is done so through a variety of means, such as stirring speeches or compelling visuals. Personal persuasion is often used as well in situations like social events. Resources can be used as weapons in the persuasion "battlefield." This means you can use what you have around you, tangible or not, to motivate people to alter their attitudes or behaviors in the manner you want. Sometimes you can use reasoning and logic to persuade, while other times you can use emotion or habit. "Systematic persuasion" is the term applied to logic and reasoning. "Heuristic persuasion" is the term for emotion and habit.

Elocution and rhetoric were the foundations of the Greek's emphasis on persuasion. Both were compelling dynamisms for persuasion. Students learned a copious amount of language to handle the many situations of communication. For example, the ancient Greek trials were determined based on the persuasion of the prosecution or defense in front of an assembly of peers. The speaker was expected to find the correct words and tools to persuade others, and this was true for whatever the circumstance.

Aristotle was the Greek philosopher who was one of the first known people to acknowledge the power and position of persuasion. He recognized its neutrality and its artistic form. He recognized that it could be used for good or bad reasons, but that it stands alone in moral alignment until enacted upon by the speaker. He broke down the necessity of learning persuasion techniques into four logical statements:

- The speaker is at fault if justice is not served within a court setting. This is because it is the speaker's job to persuade the Assembly. Justice and truth are unadulterated.
- Teaching is amplified by strong persuasion.
- Self-defense has no stronger weapon than that of persuasion.
- In order to fully comprehend a problem, it is important for a strong orator to be able to see all possible choices and contend with any eventual outcome.

Aristotle explained that the main function of persuasion is to explain a person's point of view. He also believed that reasoning and logic bred wisdom and knowledge. Because of this, Aristotle identified three methods of persuasion:

- *Pathos.* Appealing to the audience's emotions to strengthen a given position
- *Logos.* Using logic and reasoning to argue about the truth of a given statement

- *Ethos.* Demonstrating the trust and credibility of the speaker to the audience

Disagreements between human beings are bound to happen, and Aristotle understood it is because people have different perceptions of our world. These perceptions are communicated through dialogue. The challenge was how to tell whose perceptions were correct and most esteemed.

Culture

There are those who believe that being a successful persuader means being pushy or manipulative. They think they will have to force their opinions and ways of thinking onto others. This is an unfortunate cultural belief because it is not correct. Using force and manipulation may garner quick results and short-term success, however, gaining long-term influence requires more natural persuasion. This continuous influence is an implementation of scientifically based strategies carried out with integrity. They are not done with calculated tactics, intimidating others, or deceptive maneuvers. When persuasion is used to communicate truth and good intentions, people instinctively want to be persuaded by you, trust you, and believe in you. Basically, whatever you want them to do, they will do it and will do it happily.

Everyday life requires persuasion, and because of that, the discussion and cultural understanding of it changes day by day. Sometimes the conversation is misunderstood, as explained above.

Being capable of persuasion and yet not being persuaded oneself, is an evolutionary necessity and is important in everything from basic survival to cultivating wealth and success. Different cultures may require different methods of persuasion. This difference is in both how the methods of persuasion are effective and how often they are used. To provide a short example of this, advertisers will adjust the values proposed in the message depending on the culture it is being communicated to. A brand may emphasize a community-based product that brings people together in one country and emphasize individual success in another.

In the mid '90s, two researchers developed a concept called the Persuasion Knowledge Model. This concept provides a structure for analysis of the knowledge of persuasion. It also provides a method for gathering this knowledge.

"(It is necessary to include) the relationship and interplay between everyday folk knowledge and scientific knowledge on persuasion, advertising, selling, and marketing in general."

The method for communicating to the majority of people is to mix colloquial dialogue with scientific findings. This way, the general public can be educated regarding new forms of persuasion through their already established beliefs or common sense. Persuasion proficiency can become muddled when there is consistent mixing of science and folklore. The significance of proficiency can be inferred through communication like the title of a job position, scholarship accolades, or celebrity. This is how we have come to the cultural understanding that used car salesmen are not to be trusted. They are reported to use overt techniques that lead to distrust in our general culture. These techniques can range from giving the keys of the car to the customer before they have bought it to alter their perception of reality, to intertwining their personal life to the customer during the sales process.

Common Theories

There are several theories researchers have developed over the years to explain and apply persuasion to everyday life. Below are a few of those theories and a brief explanation of each one:

Attribution Theory

Human actions can be clarified by one of two attributions, situational or dispositional.

- *Situational.* This has also been referred to as "external" attribution. According to this provenance, there are certain things outside of a person's control that impact their behavior. For example, claiming a person cannot be held responsible for the situation they are in because it was bad before they became embroiled in it, is an application of situational attribution.

- *Dispositional.* This has also been referred to as "internal" attribution. The premise of this attribution is that human actions can be explained by a person's disposition, motive, traits, or abilities. For example, claiming because a person lacks certain knowledge or has a particular personality trait, such as greed or laziness, that is the reason for the current state of affairs, is an application of dispositional attribution.

Another person's behavior is most often explained or sought to be understood by dispositional attribution rather than situational. This is true because we often do not fully grasp the external or outside situations surrounding a person, so we gravitate to the complexities of the individual's internal situations. When you are trying to explain yourself or seek for others to understand you, most people will try to persuade others by using dispositional attribution to highlight their achievements and positive behaviors and situational attribution to explain their negative behaviors and inadequacies.

Conditioning Theory

Direct commands are not the actions of a strong persuader. Instead, the aim is to guide people to take their own actions. This is part of conditioning, which is a major part of persuasion. Linking a positive motivation or value to a logo of a company is an example of conditioning. Over time, the messages of joy, sexual desire, or personal connection are shown within the logo. It is an attempt to connect with the audience. Another example is in political campaigns. If a candidate makes direct face-to-face contact with potential voters, and that contact is positive, that voter is more likely to vote for that candidate. We are also conditioned to associate a certain smell or sound with an item. Think of your grandmother's house. If she was fond of baking apple pies or having rose-scented potpourri, later in life, when you smell one of those smells in an unconnected event, you will think of her. You link this with a positive emotion. This is established over time and many exposures to the message, however subtle or overt it may be.

Cognitive Dissonance Theory

Introduced in the '50s, this theory claims that humans want their thoughts, attitudes, and beliefs to be regular. Despite wanting this regularity, our cognitions can swing from alignment to disparity, or between. The disparity between your beliefs, thoughts, or attitudes is called "dissonance." This makes us uncomfortable and feeling as if we are missing something. For example, when you are diabetic and understand that eating excessively sugary foods is bad for you but do it anyways, you suffer from cognitive dissonance. Our natural inclination is to bring this dissonance into synchronization within our mind. We can bring our mental cognitions into alignment. Leon Festinger, the founder of this theory, identified four methods for creating consistent mental processes. These four steps are:

- *Change.* Our attitude, beliefs, or thoughts need to be changed.
- *Reduce.* The importance of a thought or belief needs to be condensed.
- *Increase.* The difference between the dissonance needs to be minimized, bringing the two sides closer to one another.
- *Re-evaluate.* A negotiation of the reward versus cost of the cognition needs to be reconsidered.

This means the diabetic can change their habit of eating sugary foods, reduce the impact on their health, decide they are not really at risk while eating these foods, or decide the cost of being healthy is not worth giving up the reward of the sugar-laced treat.

Functional Theories

Functional theorists attempt to understand how different situations impact the dissonance of someone's attitude regarding different objects or situations. A function that is impacted by communication can be influenced by persuasion to various degrees. Once a person is persuaded another action would fulfill the function better, the persuasion was a success. Attitudes typically have four main functions:

- *Knowledge.* Control and understand your life by setting rules and standards that will manage your sense of self.
- *Value-expressive.* We exhibit a version of ourselves that we want to align with who we want to be or what we want to believe. This exhibition gives us pleasure because it is aligned with our concept of ourself.
- *Ego-defense.* People attempt to protect their own egos from personally threatening thoughts or negative impulses. We create processes to keep ourselves from experiencing these negative scenarios.
- *Adjustment.* Decrease costs and increase affirmative exterior rewards. We choose to move from punishment to rewards with our behavior.

Inoculation Theory

This theory is just like the idea of giving a vaccine to prevent an illness that could invade the body. It may never happen, but by introducing a small amount of the virus, your body creates a defense against the disease, so if it does attack, you are prepared to fight it. To apply this to life situations, consider political parties. They may introduce an easily debunked argument to create the ability for their followers to ignore or dismiss a larger, stronger, or more developed argument from another party. Think about those negative advertisements. One political party may refute the claims of another so that when that opposite party makes those claims, the followers disregard them immediately.

Social Judgment Theory

We attempt to understand persuasive communication by sorting it subconsciously and reacting to it according to our own feelings. The attitude we already have determines how we compare and evaluate new information. This is our anchor point, or initial attitude. From this point, we decide if the persuasion falls into a realm we could accept, cannot accept, or one for which we have little interest. The closer the persuasion falls to their anchor point, the more acceptable it feels to the person.

Chapter 1.2: Putting It into Practice

"It takes tremendous discipline to control the influence, the power, you have over other people's lives."

Persuasion can be used through several various types or principles of action. Different kinds of persuasion can influence people in a variety of ways. Some people are not persuaded by emotional appeals, but rather deal with factual evidence, honoring only what can be seen and heard. On the other hand, others are driven by emotions and do not appreciate factual arguments but are willing to be persuaded with an appeal to the senses. This chapter is going to introduce some of the different types of persuasion and how to use these principles on the various people you will encounter. This chapter also introduces aids for persuasion that will help you influence others and guide them to see your point of view.

Three main types of persuasion are: "appeal to emotion," "appeal to reason," and "appeal to character." These appeals are based on Aristotle's concepts of Logos, Pathos, and Ethos.

Appeal to Emotion

How a person feels can dictate how they decide to take action. It is not based on proof or evidence. If you need to persuade a large group of people, appealing to their emotions can be more effective than using reasoning. This is because the collective population tends to be led by their emotions instead of by logic. This can be seen in examples of entire countries or civilizations making a decision based on emotion rather than logic. Faith or tradition can cause people to become emotional and make decisions for the good or detriment of their society. Imagination and pity are other emotional forms of persuasion that can be used to get someone to align with your way of thinking.

Think of the last time you test drove a car. The sales person wanted you to feel what it was like to drive behind the wheel of that exact car, so you would become more emotionally connected to it and want to repeat that feeling. Pity can be used when they are "honest" about needing the sale that month. Seduction is used in various scenarios and is most evident in forms of advertising. Think about the tagline, "There's nothing that comes between me and my Calvins."

Tradition also plays a role in persuasion. The lines, "This is the way it has always been done" or "If it isn't broke, don't fix it" or "We keep doing what we do because it is how we have always done it," are examples of this mentality. People feel that it is easier to do this than choose another method that may be available to them. Another form of tradition is considered the "bandwagon." This term is often applied to sports fans who choose to support a team because it is the popular choice at the time. You can see this type of persuasion when someone makes a comment like, "Nine times out of ten, people will choose XYZ."

Concluding an argument with an appeal to emotion is a technique that has been suggested for centuries. It reaches a person on an intimate level in order to persuade them to see your point of view. One way to conclude is with a rhetorical question that is not supposed to be answered, but rather appeals to the listener's emotional state. Think about the question, "Why wouldn't you want to feel more secure or happy?" At face value, it may appear to be an appeal to reason, but, in reality, it is to solicit an emotional response to the thought of not being secure or happy. It is an emotional persuasion technique because it does not ask the listener to actually answer the question. Images are another great way to appeal to emotion. If images are not available or feasible, using diction to describe a picture of what you are appealing to can be almost as effective.

Appeal to Reason

Logic is used in this technique to present an argument. Science and founded principles are cited. When someone is demanding proof of something, this is the best method to use. If an argument is based more on faith or feeling, people are less likely to accept it than when there is something tangible they can relate to. Scientists and mathematicians typically work in a fact-based field and make many decisions based on their observations. If you are trying to persuade them of your way of thinking, it would be best to use persuasive arguments based on fact. In addition, stating a single observation, such as what you see, is not enough of an argument for those that need an appeal to reason.

The reasoning is not a fight or disagreement. It is not heated or emotional. The argument is methodical, measured, and logical. There are two processes for reasoning: deduction and induction. Deductions are the general principles of your perception, or way of thinking. Induction is the interpretation of the facts that result in the conclusion. The conclusion is the result you are trying to persuade others to accept. Typically, a deduction has two parts: major points, and minor points. Together, these facts present the logical case to the audience.

The information you present should not be lies and should appeal to the inner reasoning of the people you are speaking with. You should aim to be effective and rational. Analytics, science, math, and academics are all good areas to draw from for an appeal. Choosing important people as sources or experts in their fields are other good resources for a reasonable argument. When you make an appeal in this manner, you have now presented a very effective means of persuasion.

Appeal to Character

This is often labeled as a person's "ethos." Through discussion and speeches, a person can be persuaded if the orator appears to be knowledgeable and kind to the listener. The person looking to persuade another must establish their character to the listener, so they can trust them. Trust is the foundation of an appeal to character.

To show that you possess a strong and trustworthy character, you should establish the following perceptions:

- *You are a reasonable person.*
- *You are in a position of authority.*
- *You live your life by a strong code of ethics.*
- *You care about the welfare of the listener.*

Another facet of appealing to the character is to make yourself appear not as an authoritative figure, but rather as a relatable and average person. Politicians do this by using terms that a typical person would use rather than political jargon.

Other Persuasion Techniques

Some techniques of persuasion are not used as frequently for various reasons. Some of the techniques are not viewed as ethical means of persuasion, while others have gained a negative opinion of the method. These techniques include:

- *Power plays.* Those in a position of power tend to automatically have followers. If a person thinks someone is powerful, they will respond to their argument more than someone they view as not having authority. Some people use the image of power or pretend to be a powerful person to persuade people to follow their direction. For example, if you are still an entry-level employee, you could pretend to be a decision maker for the company in situations outside the office to gain access to organizations or events that you otherwise would not be invited to.

- *Subliminal Messaging.* This can also be called "product placement" in movies or television. Having a product in the background of a movie or in the hands of one of the main characters tells the audience that this product is something that the character or this environment would use. The thought is that you will want to be like that person or model your home after that environment and will look to fill it with the product. Also, it is believed that the more people are exposed to a product, the more likely they will choose it when needing to make a decision related to it. Repetition of images or information encourages people to remember the information and believe in it.

- *Hypnotism.* This method requires training, but it has been shown to persuade people to do numerous things such as quit smoking or reveal their hidden desires. Typically, a person willingly submits to hypnotism; however, while being hypnotized, they are completely surrendered to the persuasion of the hypnotist.

- *Deception.* Lying and deceiving are methods of persuading people to follow you. "Fudging the numbers" or "only sharing select information" can be forms of deception because you are centering your argument on only "half-truths" and not portraying honestly the whole situation. People setting up pyramid schemes have used this effectively in the past. They set up a system to take people's money in a dishonest manner and aim to get out before they get caught in their deception.

Persuasion Aids

There are subtle things you can do to help your persuasive argument, whether it is an appeal to emotion or an appeal to reason. Four of the main aids include:

1. *Personality tests. A simple questionnaire can be filled out by employees, potential customers, or community members to share information such as how people prefer to communicate. For example, some people respond best to e-mails, while others value the connection through the telephone. Some people can be persuaded by a television commercial, while others only look for information when they need to purchase a certain item. Think about car commercials. Some people are convinced by a commercial that they need to trade in their current car for a new make or model, while others are not persuaded until they have determined they need to purchase a new car. This aid can be helpful to shed a light on a person's personality, so you can best present a persuasive argument.*

2. *Sales techniques. Honest sales techniques can be applied to various communication*

scenarios effectively. It is a tool that should not be dismissed just because some cultures view sales techniques as deceptive. It is true that some aspects are not as desirable as others, such as only communicating the good points and "ignoring" the negative aspects; however, there are some desirable skills that can be learned over time. Identifying a person's needs and explaining how your view or perspective fulfills those needs can be ethical and very persuasive.

3. *Communication skills. The stronger you grasp a culture's language, the better opportunity you have to influence them. For example, when you are writing to someone to persuade, and your letter is riddled with spelling and grammatical errors, they are less likely to take your appeal seriously. If you need to convince a room full of employees to follow a new direction that brings you all into unknown territory, but you fail to prepare a speech, you may find yourself stuttering and stammering. If your oration is peppered with "ums" and pauses, people will have less faith in your leadership. To help you improve your communication skills, you could read books, observe messages, and listen to powerful speakers for inspiration.*

> 4. *Body language. A person with crossed arms gives the appearance of being blocked and not receptive to messages. A person with their hands at their sides with open fists is more at peace and open to discussion. How you present your communication can be as persuasive as what you say, if not more so. Making eye contact, facing your body towards the person you are speaking to, and not fidgeting are all ways you can position your body to encourage people to trust and listen to you.*

NLP or Neuro-Linguistic Programming

In the 1970s, Richard Bandler and John Grinder developed an approach labeled NLP, or Neuro-linguistic programming. The concept was founded on the understanding that there is a link between the mind, language, and behavior of people. Changing one of these links can alter a person's ability to achieve their goals. This is because we observe our world subjectively. This means that we base "real" events according to our perception of what has happened rather than what has truly occurred. This perception is through our senses and the communication presented to us. Behavior is a response to these senses and perceptions. This means that simply changing the response to the perceptions and senses can change behavior. These responses can be both conscious and unconscious, and we need to learn how to train ourselves to respond differently to scenarios. This change of response is done through conditioning, often where a person is guided through a sequence or steps to come to a different conclusion or behavior. This concept has been applied to all sorts of behavior from smoking or addiction to common, everyday behaviors.

In order to use NLP to influence another person, there are certain steps that need to be taken:

- Establish a rapport with the other person.
- Gather information about the person's current state and where they want to go.
- Utilize tools and techniques to intervene and alter perceptions.
- Involve the proposed solutions in the client's life.

Rapport is established through verbal and nonverbal cues like mirroring a person's behavior or mannerisms. Body language is crucial at this stage. Once the rapport is developed, questions are asked to gather the information. These questions have both a verbal and nonverbal response that must be observed. Also, the other person needs to think beyond just obtaining their goal. They need to consider what will happen when they reach that goal. They need to consider both the positive and negative implications of their relationships when they reach their destination. Once the other person has decided this is still the direction they want to go, various persuasion techniques are used to change a person's conscious and unconscious responses, so they can obtain their goals. The final step is to create a way for the person to then experience what it is like when they have achieved that goal. This allows them to feel that success even before it has happened.

Chapter 1.3: The Six Truths of Persuasion

"To be persuasive, we must be believable; to be believable, we must be credible; to be credible, we must be truthful."

Robert Cialdini is considered one of the most influential authors on the power of influence. He was an intelligent professor who shared his insights with not just those around him but anyone willing to pick up a book and read. One of his books, *Influence,* published in 2006, is most relevant to this chapter. Throughout the book, he conducted his own research and developed six principles of influence.

The six principles he identified are based on the understanding that people can and will be influenced. It is then our job to know what and how to create that influence. The six principles are reciprocity, commitment, social proof, authority, liking, and scarcity. Understanding these principles is helpful, but what truly improves your influence is knowing how to apply them. The following sections of this chapter will identify each one and expound on how to apply them in real-life situations.

The Six Principles

Reciprocity

The premise of this principle is that when you do something nice for another person they will want to do something nice for you. It is to return the favor. This is a natural response. Even without saying it, the person on the other end of your generosity feels like they owe you. They want to pay you back for your consideration.

Commitment

When a person makes a commitment to something, no matter how big or small, they want to keep that commitment. This is especially true if the commitment is a personal one. Many times, this is because the commitments made are aligned with the ideal self-image of the person. The choice to change a behavior or thought process must align with how a person sees themself or wants to see themself.

Social Proof

People follow what those around them are undertaking. It can be small, like repeating a behavior of others because it has peaked your curiosity, or it can be large, like marching into war for a cause you do not fully understand. With the introduction of the online influence, this concept has expounded greatly. This is why websites have customer reviews and ratings and why many people make their decisions based on that information over other facts provided by the company.

Authority

Those in authority, with good or bad purpose, command influence. Most of the people in our communities are not authority figures and prefer to be led by people they view to have a relevant viewpoint, an effective communication method, and a stand from which to share their beliefs. This is a very powerful principle because of the magnitude of influence on a population.

Liking

Being liked by people not only makes us feel good, but it also means we wield incredible influence over those people. To be liked, most people have an inclination to smile and say friendly things. Looks also play a part in this principle. Good looks impact those around them. This may seem biased or unfair, but it is a factor.

Scarcity

People will seek and quickly purchase something if they think it will not be available for long. "While supplies last" or "For a limited time only" are concepts marketing uses to persuade people to take action because of this principle.

Application of the Six Principles

These six principles are what Cialdini introduced, but it is important to understand how to turn principles into actions. Below, each principle is identified with suggestions on how to apply them throughout your daily life.

Reciprocity

Offering something for free, like a professional service or a coffee for a friend, is a simple way to generate reciprocity. Here are some ideas on what to give away:

- Time. Give advice, offer to help with a task, or schedule a time for a phone call to listen to them.
- Knowledge. Help people around you by sharing your expertise on a subject. Give them the information that they need to know.
- Gifts. If you are a business, give away a sample of something to fulfill a need of the customer. If you are applying this on a personal level, give a useful gift to someone like a household item. Be considerate with the gift.
- Content. With the dawn of the internet, it has now become easier than ever to give away free content like printable forms and images, webinars, or books. Tangible content can be given as well in the form of actual books or pamphlets.

Commitment

The first step of commitment is to establish consistency or the concept of advancing your ideal self-image. To create this, it is important to understand who the other person is. Learn about how they view themselves and who they want to be. The messages you present to this other person is then biased and based on their self-image. The next step is to encourage commitment. This is a call to action. Even a small action of a person can lead to larger commitments later down the road. Here are some examples of how to ask for a small commitment:

- Social media following. This is a small connection and commitment. Gain more exposure to your brand if you are a business or to your own image if you are seeking to gain personal influence.
- Watch a video. Choosing to spend their time on watching something you have prepared for them is a small commitment and a non-threatening way to engage a person.
- Fill out a form. Giving information is a commitment to follow-up and discuss something further. Giving someone a phone number is a simple commitment. The more information they provide, like

other means of communication or their address, the more they are committing.

Social Proof

Following in the footsteps of those around you is an essential community-building tool. There are a few ways people can apply this principle:

- Testimonials. In a professional setting, this is a powerful tool. Honest and personal accounts can be easily used and shared. Personally, when a person shares their experiences with a product or service with their friends, this word-of-mouth can be more influential than any other form of marketing.
- Show off friends, especially those in common with one another. In the age of social media, it is easy to find connections that would otherwise remain under the radar. Also, if someone thinks you have plenty of connections and influence on the other people around them, they are more likely to follow you.
- Incite dialogue. If you put out content online that generates comments from other people, more people will show

interest in the content and in you. The more dialogue that occurs, the better!

Authority

You can usually establish yourself as an expert in an area as simply as proclaiming yourself as an authority. Find your position and define it clearly. Once that is completed, position yourself to be viewed as the expert in that niche. Create content, be present, and gather and give more information. This is the way to grow your position, recognition, and respect. For example, a person who enjoys riding a specific type of bike in a specific terrain can become very good at what they do on that piece of equipment. This person should then share their experiences and continue to practice, learn, and grow. Once they have established this consistently, they can then advise people on this type of bike and ride, and others will listen.

Liking

There are a variety of ways you can encourage people to like you. Some of those methods include:

- Pictures. Having people, more than one, showing their faces in a photograph with you connects people to you in a more human way. They see you as a person who is already liked by others.
- Average voice. Using a normal voice means more people understand you and will pay attention. Avoid jargon and formal diction. Do not use large and unfamiliar words. Also, when you use the first person in your writing, people connect it more personally to you.
- Be social. This means in person and online. Be active and positive. Friendly comments and presence are important and can greatly influence those around you.

Scarcity

Put yourself out there, but then bring it back by making someone feel it is only for a short time. Offer goods or a service, but restrict the quantity or time it is being offered. Some of the ways to provide scarcity include:

1. Control the numbers. Cap the quantity of an item being sold. Only order a few in each size. Explain you are only going

to give a few examples of something you are talking about.
2. Control the time. Give something an ending time or expiration point. For personal conversations, explain you only have a certain amount of time to discuss something.

This concept does not rely on reality. People just need to think there is scarcity, even if there is none, for this principle to work.

Section 2 Ultimate Influence: How to Use Conversation to Persuade in Any Circumstance

"Rhetoric may be defined as the faculty of observing in any given case the available means of persuasion. This is not a function of any other art."

In your personal and professional life, how much do you control the conversations? This is one way to consider your influence over other people. There are four pillars to influence in communication: the power of position, emotional control, topic expertise, and control over the connection.

Your power of position will be one of the easiest ways to have influence. People with more real or perceived power will have more influence. However, people with power tend to talk more than others, interrupt conversations, and force the conversation to go in certain directions, thus damaging the power of their position. A person who controls their power by engaging in meaningful dialogue can be even more influential.

Emotional control is critical. Letting your emotions run your conversation can be detrimental to your influence, but allowing emotion to pepper your argument or persuasion can be powerful. Think about how best to show your passion for your point of view or way of thinking and use it wisely. Sometimes, a well-placed expletive or watery eye can showcase how deeply you feel about what you are speaking about. Sobbing or turning red while cursing is the opposite. No matter how much of an expert you are on a topic, being too emotional can degrade your authority quickly.

Passion links well with expertise. When a person is knowledgeable and well prepared and also passionate, they are an almost unstoppable force of influence. This is especially helpful if you are not in the position of power in the conversation. It is the terrible truth that experts can be ignored if they cannot communicate their knowledge well, and people with little experience can be followed because they can sway a crowd with a stirring oration. This is another reason why communication is so powerful and needs to be honed.

The final pillar of influence in communication includes controlling the connection. It is not the most powerful pillar, but it is important. This is not just through conversation and verbal information but over your body language and understanding how others are presenting themselves

When you are dedicated to communicating with people, you need to be aware of these pillars of influence and how you can control almost any situation with the correct words or actions. The following chapters are here to guide you in understanding how different conversational tactics can provide you with the ultimate influence in any scenario. Topics such as creating a magnetic personality, how to greet someone and make small talk, and how to listen all lead into understanding how to effectively communicate with others.

Chapter 2.1: Magnetism Is Not Magical: How to Create a Magnetic Personality

"Character may almost be called the most effective means of persuasion."

Many people seek to develop a personality that attracts others to them. This attraction could be for romantic purposes, professional advancement, or personal friendships. The difficult thing about creating this personality is that it requires an honest self-evaluation and mental persuasion. We have internal barricades that we have either intentionally or unintentionally erected that prevent us from developing the connections we are truly seeking. For example, not being able to find the right words in a discussion or feeling uncomfortable speaking with people are types of internal barricades. You need to tear these down so that you can begin improving your conviction.

Those we choose to surround ourselves with also provide a form of communication to others about who we are. When we value ourselves and surround ourselves with others who value themselves, the magnetic and positive energy is apparent. In addition, if you find yourself doubting your greatness, the successful people around you will knowingly or unknowingly encourage you to push yourself to be better. You become more successful, and your personality becomes more "attractive" to others.

To find success with a magnetic personality, you need to overcome low self-esteem and become confident in yourself. Not believing in yourself is crippling and leads to many negative traits. Changing this one area can ultimately change many aspects of your life and draw people to you naturally. This does not mean you need to change who you are, but rather how you view yourself as you are. Once you accept your unique traits, you will begin to grow in confidence. You should not fear or regret being who you are and instead should seek out the magnetic qualities you already embody. Ask yourself what makes people speak or interact with you. This could be in any situation. Identify situations or scenarios where people spoke and listened to you and why they did so. One of the most common scenarios where people will listen to you and seek you out is when you get them to speak for themselves, and they feel good. People associate feeling good and value with speaking to you and, therefore, want to be around you all the time. They like that feeling and want more of it! Then, when they speak about you to others, they are in turn letting them know how you make them feel. Now, others want to meet and interact with you.

What are some of the practical tips on how to create this connection and get others to feel you are listening to them? How can you make them feel good about themselves? Follow a few of these tips and you will begin to see almost immediate magnetism:

1. When someone you know puts something out there in the world, such as a book, a blog post, or a photograph, you can easily make him or her feel good by offering a thoughtful comment or review. This is especially effective if the person is new at their public endeavor. It is a quick and easy way to show you care about what they are doing and value their contributions.

2. Sending a personal note to someone, either by mail, email, or text, letting someone know how they have impacted your life can make a large impact. It makes that person feel good about their connection to you, and it makes them want to do something nice for you in return.

3. Friendship can be taken for granted, and we often forget to thank our friends for being a meaningful part of our world. A simple show of gratitude can mean a lot to someone, especially when most people are caught up in the excess information prevalent in our communities. This is a social relationship that is often taken for granted. Again, surrounding yourself with positive and valuable friends raises you up and draws even more success to you. This relationship should always be fostered.

4. Do not underestimate the impact of social media. Many people participate on social sites like Facebook and Instagram to receive positive feedback. Writing something kind and thoughtful to someone on these sites outside of the traditional birthday wish is not only validating to them but to all those that view them as a friend. The positivity that you share can become contagious, and others will want you to share some of that consideration with them. They will seek your comments.

5. Choose your compliments well. Do not say something nice if you do not mean it;

however, seek to find something special to compliment a person on. Also, do not offer a compliment and use it to expect something in return. This is evidently insincere. Be honest and thoughtful in bestowing a compliment on someone, and they will feel valued and positive.

6. Sometimes people talk about energy or vibes, and a lot of people may roll their eyes or dismiss this as nonsense; but, the reality is, being positive and enthusiastic in life are apparent to others, even if you never speak to them. When you are confident in yourself and are striving to be a magnetic human, others will notice in your actions, body language, the tone of your voice, mannerisms, and more. These traits will draw others to you subconsciously, just like the opposite traits will repel people.

7. Participate in activities that make you feel good and that involve other people. For example, if you love video games, go to a place that allows others to play video games with you. If you love to run, join a running club. When you are having fun and feeling good around others who also love that activity, you are associating them with that feeling of

enjoyment, but they are also associating you with that feeling. Think about the first time you accomplished something you have wanted to do or try, such as surfing or water skiing. When you finally stood up on the board or skis, think about the people that were there with you teaching and encouraging you. That surge of adrenaline and joy are now connected to those people as well as to the event.

Chapter 2.2: Steps to Making Casual Conversation

"That's all small talk is - a quick way to connect on a human level - which is why it is by no means as irrelevant as the people who are bad at it insist. In short, it's worth making the effort."

The fear of talking to someone you have never met, or know nothing about, can bring up anxiety in even the most confident and outgoing person. But being able to communicate and form meaningful connections is vital to creating happiness and strong human bonds. The thought of surface conversations may not seem to fulfill this desired link; however, it is not fake or a waste of time. This does not mean that you should only talk about unimportant matters like the weather or the food. People seek deeper conversations that are meaningful. This is because we are social and constantly seek meaning. We want our lives to mean something. Getting into this type of conversation is not always stress-free and does not always flow with ease. Think about the last time you were in an awkward conversation with someone when a person you were trying to talk to did not want to or did not seem capable of responding back. Or have you ever felt trapped in a conversation you have no interest in? Having strong small-talk skills can help you turn these situations around and leave you and your communication partner fulfilled and happy.

The purpose of this chapter is to provide a how-to guide for making small talk that is both meaningful and bonding. Break the ice, create new relationships, and grow professionally. The more you practice this skill, the more comfortable you will become with it.

Step 1: Use body language and a friendly tone to set the foundation of the conversation.

Sincere eye contact, well-placed nodding, and leaning your body into the other person are all good forms of body language that communicate to the other person that you are engaged and are listening. A polite smile, open arms, and attention are all important. Not having welcoming body language can shut down a conversation before it even starts.

If you can, turn your whole body towards the person you are talking to. Be mindful that this stance and leaning towards them is friendly and does not feel forceful or threatening. Other useful tips include:

- Put away your cell phone. Do not check your email or messages when trying to connect with someone in front of you. Even just having your phone out can distract from the conversation. Put it out of sight if you can. If you are at dinner or a networking event with a table, do not place it on the table. If you need to keep your phone out because of an important call or email, let the person know that this is the reason for the presence of the phone. This way they know you are not using it as a way to avoid talking with them.

- Be careful not to seem overly eager. Do not lean in too far that they feel intruded upon. Do not scare them by never breaking eye contact. If you try to talk to someone when you are in their personal bubble, they will reject the conversation instead of wanting to engage in it.

If you know the person you are about to speak with, use their name in a friendly way, such as, "Hi, Tom, it's nice to see you." If you do not know the person, consider another friendly greeting like, "Hi, my name is Alison. What is your name?" When they reply with their name, make sure to use it. Some people suggest finding a way to say it three times in the early conversation, so it is committed to your memory. Use this in conjunction with good body language to make the person feel special and not like a nuisance or a placeholder until others arrive.

Focus on keeping the topics of conversation light, positive, and fun. Try to laugh easily and have a smile ready at a moment's notice. This is relevant even if you have had a bad day. This person is not a close confidant yet, so it is best to not overwhelm them or shut them out by being negative. Negativity turns most people off immediately, especially when they do not know you.

If you struggle with what to say after the initial greeting, offer a sincere and unique compliment followed by a question about it. For example, "Wow, you have a stunning pair of earrings. What a beautiful accent piece to your outfit. Where did you find them?" This is especially great if you want to direct them to a topic of shopping, but it can just simply open the door to a conversation. It opens the door with grace because it makes the person feel appreciated and noticed. If you do not want to introduce yourself first, you can start with the compliment and then move into a friendly greeting.

Step 2: Begin the conversation on common ground and without saying much.

Now that contact has been made, you can begin actually speaking to one another. There are a few different ways you can start this conversation beyond those first few introductory remarks. For example, you can find out if you have something in common with the other person. This can be about anything, big or small. It is okay to begin small here. Weather can be a good introduction as long as it leads to topics that matter to you and the other person. Think of comments like, "Don't you think this presentation is so informative?" or "Wasn't that snow storm this afternoon so crazy?" or "This restaurant serves the best bacon." Once you gain a link to common ground you can then move forward by exposing something about yourself.

This is an intimate gesture that lets the other person drop their guard a bit. Do not feel you need or should share something too personal. That will backfire on your intention of connection. Instead, try something like, "I have actually been coming to these sessions for years now and always find out something new." or "I was trying to go to the gym to work out today but had to try to do some things at home instead. It was awful!" or "Every time I come to this restaurant I order an extra side of it to take home for the next day. It's like treating myself to another breakfast out but in the comfort of my PJs."

Once you have demonstrated that you are willing to share personal information about yourself, you should invite the other person to add to the conversation. This is the time to ask a lot of questions, but remember, steer clear of "heavy" topics. This is meant to be a light and fun conversation. Things like religion or politics can get somber quickly and negate the purpose of the small talk. When you ask your questions, keep them open-ended, meaning you are phrasing them in a way that encourages the person to respond with a sentence rather than a yes or a no. Typically, open-ended questions begin with a "why" or "how." "What" questions tend to garner short and simple replies. Aim to grow the conversation with the questions you ask rather than narrow it down.

Other questions to avoid are the typical ones like, "What do you do?" or "Where are you from?" These are stock questions and do not show the interest you have in the other person. Be curious about them and try to build on the common ground you found earlier. Do not ask "How was your day?" but rather "Did anything exciting happen to you today?" or "What happened in your day today?" Once the person is talking, listen to what they have to say and ask more questions about it. Be interested!

Following the above examples regarding an information session, snowfall, or bacon, follow up questions can be, "Have you come to other sessions, or is this your first time? The others I attended were good, but this one has been really great!" or "Did the snow keep you from doing anything this afternoon?" or "What do you come to this restaurant for? Is it for the bacon, too, or for the awesome coffee?" These all seek to expand on the common ground and ask the other person to provide their own opinions in a safe conversation.

Another form of engagement can be to ask for advice. Many people love to talk about themselves and what they have done. It makes the other person feel good and validated. Asking advice can sound like, "Have you attended other programs outside of this company? What are your thoughts on how this one is presented?" or "How do you get in a workout when you are home-bound? I struggle with staying motivated and focused," or "Do you have other favorite restaurants in the area? I'm always on the hunt for other great options!"

After you initiate the engagement and response from the other person, you need to decide how you will respond to keep the conversation expanding and going. This means, after the person responds to your initial question, you need to ask another question or reply with your own statement. Sometimes a well-placed and appropriate joke can be relevant. Be careful with jokes. Keep them politically correct and light-hearted. "Dad" jokes like silly knock-knock jokes or puns can be good in your communication repertoire. Also, be cautious with the questions you are asking. Do not make the other person feel like they are in an interrogation. Keep sharing bits about yourself with the conversation, so it is a true dialogue, back and forth.

Think about your response as a natural inquisition or connection. You could respond something like, "That is awesome you have been able to attend so many other great programs. What was your favorite one?" or "That sounds like a great method for working out at home. How did you discover that? Do you follow someone or something online?" or "I have tried that restaurant as well. Some people claim it is a little stuffy, but I do not agree."

Once the conversation begins going back and forth, observe what is around you, including more of the other person. This could be something they are wearing or something within the room that you think would apply to both of you. This way if the topic at hand wears out, you can have something lined up to introduce next.

Most of the banter should be back and forth, with you inquiring and the other person talking. Try to do more of the listening and less of the talking. Asking the person, "Tell me more," is like a magic bullet to open up the other person and get them sharing. This also allows you to sit back and really listen. Remember to watch their verbal cues to make sure they are still engaged in the topic and conversation. Rephrase the conversation of the other person and reflect on the comments to show you are truly paying attention. When replying to their questions, share details, not just surface information. This gives the other person personal information to work with as well.

When you actually listen to the other person's comment, you may pick up on other common grounds you could use to steer the conversation towards. Be careful not to take over the conversation and change the topic without waiting for an appropriate time to do so. For example, when someone responds to your question by saying, "I live in downtown New York because I love the West Side. The energy there is addictive." You could respond with, "That is why I chose to live in the heart of my city as well; there is nothing like the bustle of all that activity. My favorite thing to do is to watch people walking down the sidewalk and imagine what they do for work or where they are going." This allows the other person to elaborate on your comment or share more about what energy they like in their neighborhood.

Step 3: Bring the conversation to a close with grace and a follow-up plan.

As you recognize the conversation is nearing an end, like when the music is about to start, the break is coming to a close, or the event is ending, make sure you have shared something personal about yourself. This means something you are passionate about but nothing that is too much for a first conversation. Those more sensitive topics can wait until a deeper bond has been developed. In a small talk connection, you want the person to feel they have connected and not been filler for a time slot.

If you are interested and feel the connection was good, you can mention getting together again. It is not inappropriate to tell the other person that you enjoyed talking with them about the topics you covered and would like to talk more. Ask for their contact information. If you do not feel comfortable, encourage or mention a place you both visit for the opportunity to meet again. Try phrasing things like, "I am really looking forward to that movie premier and would love to go with someone who is equally as excited. Can I get your number, so we can go together?" or "It is so refreshing to meet someone who loves bacon as much as I do. I like to host a potluck once a month and would love for you to come to try some of the different concoctions we come up with, and for you to share your own. Can I get your contact information, so I can send you the details?" or "Maybe I'll see you at the coffee shop in the neighborhood sometime. I hear they are doing a story time on Tuesday mornings. It would be fun for our kids to get together while we grab a cup."

Finish the conversation clearly and thoughtfully. Let them know you loved speaking with them, wish you could talk longer, or you want to introduce them to another person you think they would connect with.

Chapter 2.3: It All Starts with 'Hello'

"You've probably noticed how when someone says hello or smiles at you, your automatic reaction is to say hello or smile back."

Why Should You Smile?

Emotions are powerful motivators. People make decisions based on their emotions most of the time. For example, if someone feels nervous about something, they will be more aware of how they handle themselves or things around them. They may place more importance on seemingly unimportant things. On the other end, you do not always know how someone is feeling until you talk to him or her. That first impression of you can either lower or heighten the emotion of the other person. The difference between making a meaningful connection with someone and creating a gap between the two of you can boil down to this first contact. The best way to create a positive first impression? Smile. And then say, "Hello."

People become more comfortable when they are greeted with a friendly smile. If the greeting can be personal, it can go even further to calming someone down or cheering them up. The greeting can be personalized by simply adding their name. It can be personalized further by adding a unique compliment to them or engaging in small talk that is based on common ground between you and the other person. Make the person the center of attention as quickly as possible. This helps you build trust and rapport.

Another component is the tone of your voice. Be congenial and kind. Mean what you say when you say hello. Do not write off this powerful moment of connection as unimportant. Make it powerful with importance. Enjoy the contact and camaraderie.

Saying hello to someone is not a burden. It is a common contact that we do on a daily basis with all sorts of people. It is a natural part of communication. This is why it should be done sincerely and with thought. It is also why it is one of the simplest methods of showing your earnestness. How can you do this easily? Smile. And then say, "Hello."

To be ready to greet people in such a friendly and cheerful manner, it is important to be prepared mentally for this task. This means being in a good mood. If you are not, or are experiencing bad circumstances, try to put yourself in a happy place by thinking of a positive experience or memory before you know you will be meeting another person. Before you interact with another person, take a deep breath and think positive thoughts. This calm and positive nature will come through in your facial expressions and tone of your voice. The people you meet will feel comfortable and trusting.

If the outside situations or your mood are too bad, and you cannot change into a positive attitude, pretend like you have. Plaster a smile on your face despite how you feel. It can sometimes be effective and influence the environment around you. It has also been proven to improve your own mood.

Saying hello with a bright smile can transform a client who only purchases every now and again into a loyal regular, turn someone's mood from sadness or frustration to a brighter outlook, and diffuse a tense situation between people. Recognize this power and feel it when someone smiles and says hello to you. It is not a magic bullet. It is a natural trait that we can use to make a major influence at the start of any connection.

Why Should You Say Hello?

The greeting is a powerful tool that jump-starts a good conversation. It opens the door to a personal connection which all humans need. The friendly greeting of a "Hello" and a smile can put a stranger at ease and set the connection up for success. The first impression you make on someone will be dependent a lot on your greeting. The same goes for your first impression of them!

A greeting can be considered an introduction to a large group of people as well as to an individual. When you are giving a speech, that first minute of your talk sets the tone of your influence. It captivates the people's interest and attention. The opinion of your speech from these people will rest on how well you do in that first minute of your greeting and introduction.

When someone knocks on your door or calls you on the phone, people expect you to greet them because it is considered common courtesy. It does not matter who the person is that calls or stops by. You are expected to greet them with a friendly greeting. In fact, when the phone rings or the doorbell sounds, we often drop what we are doing, no matter if we are in the middle of something or not, and rush to greet that person. This expectation of attention and kindness should be a common courtesy in all your greetings.

A thoughtful, personal greeting that makes the other person or people feel special is valid because those people are important. They should be treated as such. Think of a customer to your business. They are literally funding your dreams; treat them that way. Think of a friend who is being considerate and stopping by to see you. They are showing you how they care about you and your situation; treat them that way. If you do not greet someone, they feel ignored and neglected. It feels good to at least be acknowledged!

If a greeting is to be the most effective, it should be personal and sincere. There are some key components to making someone feel like they are truly being greeted:

- Wow them right away. The first ten seconds of an interaction can be all you get to make an impression in a personal setting. In a speech to a group of people, you get about 60. If you fail to greet the person with a friendly hello within this time frame, you will have damaged that first impression. This does not mean they will never be won over to your point of view or value you as a friend, but it does mean you have now set yourself up for a more challenging battle of persuasion. If a person feels ignored, they will probably look elsewhere for a conversation or influence.

- Look them in the eye. If you do not bother to look up at someone when you say hello you might as well not even say it. Same goes for addressing a crowd. If you have your head down and are staring at your notes, or your shoes, or are looking over your shoulder, people will feel you are dismissing them and that they are not worth the common courtesy of a proper greeting. They feel disrespected. Lifting your head, bringing your eyes to focus on them, and having a soft and friendly gaze go a long way in making a person feel validated.

- Do not forget to smile. If you say hello to someone without a smile, even if it is fake and they know it, they will feel this greeting is just a requirement, and you do not care about them. A fake smile is better than no smile, even though it does not pack the same punch. This component of the greeting is so important that it warrants its own section in this chapter! Pair a cheerful "Hello" with a smile and you have now established a strong introduction.

- Make it personal. Using someone's name when you know it makes a person feel like they belong in that conversation and that they are special. Hearing your name, in a personal or professional setting, is something most people love to hear. In addition, recalling something about them, such as a funny story, a common purchase, or a previous action, can go a long way in establishing the feeling that you care about them and value them as a person. If you forget someone's name, you can get around this by using phrasing like, "It's good to see you again." This makes the person still feel like you recognize them despite not being very personal.

- Mix it up. If you say the same thing to everyone all the time, people will catch on quickly that you are not really paying attention to them. The first couple of encounters you may be able to get away with, but people will eventually realize you are not being sincere. Using your observations, customize your greeting to the person you are talking to. For example, if the AC is out in the auditorium of people you are addressing, acknowledge that by saying, "Good afternoon, thank you to everyone who is here today. I know it is uncomfortable without the air conditioning, and it means a lot to me that you have chosen to stay to listen to my message. Please do not hesitate to get a drink of water throughout my speech to keep yourself cooler." This is a far better greeting than something like, "Good afternoon, thank you for being here." Also, for personal greetings, mix up how you say hello. Think about where the person had to come from to get there, or what is going on that led them to you.

- Do not forget about yourself. People may not already know who you are, or they may have forgotten. By introducing yourself, you let the person know how to address you and drive the conversation to a more personal level, not just a surface interaction.

- Respect the bubble. People have an invisible bubble of personal space. When someone crosses into the bubble, knowingly or unknowingly, it can make him or her feel uncomfortable. It puts them on edge because they view this as an attack on their personal safety, even if it is a friendly contact. A good rule of thumb is to stand about three feet from the other person and only occasionally interact closer than that when necessary. A handshake is not considered an intrusion into the bubble if it is expected. A hug can be too much. An arm around the shoulder or a whisper in the ear can be too intimate for general acquaintances. Give them space.

- The best policy is honesty. If you can, always be sincere in your greeting. Be genuine. When you fake it, especially if you fake it all the time, people will recognize this and be turned off. If you have to fake a friendly greeting, do not be afraid to explain why you are having a hard time briefly. Use a comment such as, "Hi. I'm sorry I'm a little off, I had a rough time getting here, but I am excited to be able to meet you."

When someone perceives you as friendly, and you make them feel special, valued, important, and that they belong, people will want to listen to you and come back to you.

Chapter 2.4: How Listening Is a Form of Persuasion

"The art of conversation is the art of hearing as well as of being heard."

— William Hazlitt, Selected Essays, 1778-1830

Can you distinguish the difference between hearing and listening? Some people think that there is no difference between the two, but being an "active" listener is very different than just observing someone is speaking words in your general area. The concept of "active" listening is an exchange technique where the listener must respond to the speaker by replying to what was said by rephrasing what they heard. It shows that both people understand each other. Each word the person says is heard, and the listener is clear on what has been communicated to them. The listener is not thinking about anything other than what is being said. This listening skill is what builds quality relationships.

Listening to someone when they talk to you is more than just being polite or kind. It holds a lot of weight to the person's opinion of you and how you value them. Listening can also accomplish a lot of things in your efforts to persuade them to see your point of view or to do something different. To be a good persuader, you need to be a good listener.

Why Is It Important to Listen?

The majority of this book has been centered around how to communicate with others to persuade them to follow you, to change their perspective on a topic, or to make them do something different. You use your words and body language to get them on your side and have influence over them. So how does not talking and letting them speak accomplish this? There are a few reasons.

First of all, people trust you more when they feel they can share with you. If a person feels that they can talk openly about things with you and that you will listen to what they have to say, they trust you more. They see that you value their point of view. Trust is the cornerstone to influence and establishing your character. Listening is the easiest method to gain that trust. When a person realizes you are willing to listen to them and you are encouraging them to talk, your credibility goes up. And this is not only with the person you are speaking to, but all the people witnessing the conversation. People want to be heard, and when they see someone is willing to do that, they want to be the next to talk. They see a listener as capable and competent. They view you as wanting to work with them and not against them. You are not telling them how to do something without first listening to how it is being done already. Imagine if someone you are speaking to is upset about something. Simply opening your ears and listening to them can show your empathy and support. They feel they are important enough to be listened to. You subconsciously are telling them that you respect them, and they are important. What a powerful connection!

As a psychologist, the majority of my role is to listen to people. There are many times I do not say more than a few words to people. Yet, despite my silence, my clients trust me and come back week after week. They know I value them and think what they say and do is important. I demonstrate this to them through my listening, not just because I have training in how to help them.

I am able to help my clients by listening to the information they provide me and make mental notes about important details. I can do my job because they gave me a lot of information to work with. The questions I ask or the comments I make are there as a guide to get people to open up and share about themselves. This also encourages them to drop their guard a little bit. If I did not spend the time listening to them, why should they spend the time listening to me?

Think about an exchange with a person recently where you felt they jumped in too soon with their perspective and thoughts. Did you feel engaged, valued, and understood? This could be a friend or colleague or a sales person who does not take the time to listen. Consider how it made you feel when you thought they weren't listening to you. Have you ever asked someone a question, and they seemed to be ignoring you or they did not answer it? Instead of bonding, do you feel disconnected? You cannot get what you need to get done if you do not have a connected audience to listen to you. Listen to them, and they will listen to you.

8 Tips on How and Why to Be a Better Listener

- People fall into the trap of misunderstanding the power of listening. They do not see the benefit or reward of listening to another person, especially when they have an agenda. But the theory of reciprocity applies to listening. If you show you are actively listening to another person, they will be more likely to listen to you in return. If you focus on understanding, they will, too.

- Keep in mind that part of active listening is to be able to recall the conversation and information later to show you understood what was communicated. Stay alert and ask questions or for information to be repeated, so you make sure the information sticks in your mind. This also helps you stay in the moment and stop thinking about what to talk about next. The information that you will recall is powerful. After all, "Knowledge is power." The person talking is giving away information, and the person listening is gaining it. By listening, you are gaining more power.

- Staying focused on the person is critical. This means keeping your eyes focused on them the majority of the time. Aim to increase the amount of time you make eye contact in conversations and focus on their eyes. When the person feels that you are paying attention to them they feel cared for and understood. This is a valuable feeling to people and something that is not common in today's society.

- Remove distractions if possible. This includes your phone or computer. Multi-tasking is not possible when you are trying to listen, because you need to be completely present in the conversation. Browsing the internet or reading an email will make you miss some of what the other person is saying, not to mention the negative impact it has on eye contact. If you need to use it during the conversation to check something or note something related to the conversation, let them know that. For example, say, "That's an interesting question, and I am not sure about that. Let me look it up quickly," or "I need to write that down. That is great insight!"

- Recall what is said by paraphrasing the information. Just a few seconds to recall some of the main points you just heard not only confirms that you heard the information correctly, but it also shows the other person that you really were listening to them. This gives the other person the opportunity to correct something you said to make sure it is accurate. The summary also sets the tone for sharing your perspectives or questions appropriately. The summary is not an assumption, but rather a confirmation of the information just provided to you. Active listening requires observation but not mind-reading. Do not assume anything based on something the other person said or did. Ask questions to clarify the information.

- A clear and present mind is needed. Being tired or distracted makes it almost impossible to listen well to another person. Take a walk outside to get some air or do some exercises to keep your mind and focus sharp.

- Listening can be hard when you want to relate to another person. You want to share your experiences, and sometimes you feel like if you just input a little information about yourself, the other person will feel more connected to you from this common ground. This is not the case. Do not interrupt or jump in. Do not offer solutions if the person is not asking for them. Do not take over the conversation talking about your situation that was similar to theirs unless they ask. Just listen until they are done talking. Some people just need to vent and do not need a solution. They will probably arrive at it on their own. Let them talk. This also allows you to not share something you wish you had not. You cannot take back information once you say it; use it wisely. Wait until it is the right time to share a common ground or offer advice. It will be more powerful when used thoughtfully later.

- Know when enough is enough, and you cannot take anymore. If you are tired, stressed, or in a hurry, you need to let the other person know because it will affect your ability to listen to them. If a friend calls you and needs to be heard, let them know that you need to start dinner in 30 minutes, or you have an appointment you need to leave for by 4 PM. Also, if you have been listening and trying to stay present but notice you are starting to wander, let the person know you need to take a break. Maybe use the restroom to decompress or get something to eat or drink. It is okay to step back and process before being a present listener again. There is a reason there is a time limit to psychiatry sessions! Being honest about your ability to listen is better for the relationship than trying to fake it. Also, by being honest you can prevent yourself from saying something you do not really mean or that is not appropriate. A thoughtless comment can cause irrevocable damage to the relationship.

Show You Are Listening and Not Just Hearing Noise

This is a practice that takes time and effort. Calming your mind and focusing on just the speaker is a challenge when there are so many distractions around us that we cannot control. We also have our own need to communicate and be listened to. If the topic of the speaker is something we do not value ourselves or find interesting, the process of actively listening can be even harder. Avoid the temptation to stop the conversation or change the subject. Practice your skills in any situation, so when you need to use them to gain maximum influence over a person or group of people, you can be effective and persuasive.

It is important to note that active listening is not a stepping-stone to an argument. It is a way to understand another person. If you do not agree with their viewpoint, ask more questions to see why they think or behave that way. The more you understand, the more credible you will be, and when you do begin to use influence over their thoughts or behaviors, they are more likely to follow your direction because you understood them and are speaking to them personally rather than on a surface level. Encouraging them to share upfront allows you to get all the information you need to persuade them without begging for it or trying to get it out of them later.

To show someone you empathize with what they are saying, nod your head. A well placed "Yes" or "Uh-huh" can be a quick way to illustrate that you are listening and understand them. Body language plays an important role in communicating without using words. Other phrases like, "Go on," "Tell me more," "Wow," "Great!" or "Interesting" all show you're listening and interested. To make sure you understood what was said, ask questions that begin with, "What I understand then is that....?" or "So what you are saying is...." or "What I just heard you say is...." or "What do you mean by....?" These are other ways to ask clarifying questions to show that you are listening and to make sure the information you are taking in is accurate.

Chapter 2.5: What to Do When People Do Not Listen: How to Handle Conflict

"Conflict is drama, and how people deal with conflict shows you the kind of people they are."

-Stephen Moyer

Conflict is inevitable when you are seeking to understand and persuade others. Different goals, personalities, and opinions all influence how we respond to information, and emotions can cloud judgment. Being able to handle conflict, getting people to listen to you, and communicating with those that disagree with you are all skills that take time to master but are some of the strongest traits you can develop for persuasion and influence.

Resolve Conflict in 5 Steps

When you do get into a disagreement with someone, whether it is a heated argument or a passive disagreement, it is important that you handle it well to keep the relationship intact. Below are five steps you can use to find and resolve just about any disagreement:

- Find the cause. This means the more information you have about why the conflict began, the better chance you have of resolving it. Ask questions to find out where the disagreement began. Questions like, "When did you begin feeling this way?" or "How did this problem begin?" Encourage people to open up and be honest about how they feel. If you are mediating a disagreement between two people, let each person tell their side of the story without interruption. This lets both parties know that you are impartial to the conflict and want to find an amicable solution.

- Life does not happen in a vacuum. Understand that just one incident does not lead often to conflict. Typically, there are other factors at play. Something could have happened earlier between the two that has now festered to a boiling point. Or you may have triggered an old wound a person is nursing without realizing it. It is important to look outside and beyond the current conflict to understand what the true cause of conflict is. Questions like, "What do you think caused this to happen?" or "When do you think this conflict first arose?" help you find the root of the issue, not just the conflict at hand.

- Involve the others in finding a solution. Do not assume you know how to fix a problem, whether it is between you and another person, or between two people you are talking with. Once the person has shared their thoughts on why and how a conflict arose, ask them how they see it being resolved. It may be completely irrational or illogical. It can even still be hurtful language or ideas, but it is important you give the other person the opportunity to offer a solution to fix the relationship. The goal of this is to get the other person to stop being defensive and start thinking about working together. Try asking a question such as, "How can we make this better between us?"

- Once the other person offers a solution or two, discuss what you think would be an acceptable solution if they did not already mention it. Make sure to summarize the solutions the other person offered and identify the benefits of each of their solutions. Do the same with your suggestion if you offered one as well. Involve them in the discussion about what would be best for the two of you or the group. Sometimes a solution is not great for either person, but it is the best for the organization or group. It is important to note this and find a way both people can support it.

- After a solution is identified that both people can support, each person needs to agree on how they are going to move forward after the conflict. Shaking hands typically solidifies this. Asking questions like, "What actions are you going to take to prevent conflicts in the future?" or "What do you plan to do if a conflict arises again?" can help make sure you know how the other person plans on addressing a problem moving forward.

These steps work well with someone who is willing to communicate and listen, but what if they are not open to listening to your point of view?

How to Get Them to Listen

When you are trying to communicate something, maybe a different perspective, instructions, or advice, it can be frustrating when the other person is not willing to listen to you. Despite your best efforts, some people are bad listeners. They may choose to not listen, or they just do not know how to. There are two things you can do in this situation: give up and walk away or keep trying to communicate with them. If you are trying to persuade someone, you need to be able to communicate with them. In order to communicate, they need to listen to you. This means, if you decide you really want this non-listener to be influenced by you, you need to stick it out and find a way for them to communicate with you.

Not all non-listeners are doing it intentionally, and you do need to be patient while they find their way to trusting in your words. Sometimes they need to make a small mistake, so they listen to you before making a large one. Think about children, they often learn by making mistakes. If you provide guidance to them about not jumping off the couch because it can hurt them, they may not listen. When they do hurt their elbow or knee, they will put it together that you were right. This means when you advise them not to jump off from the roof onto the trampoline, there is a stronger likelihood they will listen to you because you were right before, and they did not listen.

There are other times people will not listen and you cannot understand why. Maybe they feel they know more than you, or they do not like to admit they are wrong. Sometimes they are defensive about change or different ideas. In my experience, some of the best ways to deal with people who do not or cannot listen include:

- Ask more questions and get their perspective on the topic at hand. Forcing them to talk about a subject will begin to open them up to a conversation.

- Consider approaching the topic in a different way or with different language. Maybe they do not like the tone of voice you used, or the language was confusing to them. Rephrase what you are saying to see if that engages them better.

- Reflect on how you presented information. Did you sound like you were barking orders instead of providing guidance? Were you acting like a know-it-all instead of a confidant? Adjust if needed.

- Do not dismiss someone's emotions as unimportant. If something you said made them angry or upset, do not belittle them by saying, "You should not be angry." Instead, find out why they feel that way about what you said and explain your stance in a manner that is personal to them.

- Avoid trying to force someone to do or say something. Be understanding of a person's place in the relationship and conversation. Allow them to feel how they feel and think the way they think before trying to alter their perceptions. Applying force is a poor form of persuasion. Guiding them to find the answer on their own typically prevents conflicts and opens doors to communicate.

- Do not underestimate different communication methods. Sometimes, it is not the right time or place to speak to someone about something. They may be busy, stressed, or tired. If they need to be able to revisit your communication, consider writing it down. If you want them to emotionally connect with what you are saying, try involving a visual aid of some sort. Graphs, charts, or pictures can be powerful. If they seem distracted, set a time for them to have the conversation. Setting a time and place aside to talk can be a powerful tool in getting them to listen to you.

- Allow silence to exist. Do not feel the need to jump in and fill a void, especially if you are talking about an important or difficult subject. Some people just need time to think about their response, and your constant speaking can distract or discourage them from trying to engage with you.

- Find a tool to make them more comfortable with you. Think about children and needing a blankie to hold in unfamiliar situations. Provide a "blankie" to the person you are talking to. This could be a favorite snack or drink, a comfortable chair, or an intimate room.

How to Talk to People Who Disagree with You

There will come a time when you need to disagree with someone. Despite all your powers of persuasion, you will need to debate something. Writing a well-crafted argument can seem like the best and most effective approach, but in reality, the best way to persuade someone is in person. This means that they either watch something you have prepared, or you speak with them directly about it. This method of communication makes the other person view your argument as more valid and your character stronger than if you wrote it down. The tone of voice and body language are factors in this interpretation. Also, the written word takes the humanity from you, and opens up the opportunity for the other party to belittle your intelligence or moral character. It may sound harsh, but when emotions come into a disagreement on important topics, this is a subconscious maneuver we all are naturally inclined to.

In order to communicate with someone you openly disagree with, stay visible as much as possible and follow these steps:

- Use the other person's perspective to begin your conversation. Identify what you disagree on, such as politics or religion, and state what that person's beliefs are. Then use that to discover why they made those decisions. For example, if someone believes gun control is irrelevant, but you think it is important, start with their perspective and find out why they think there should be less control.

- Take the time to be there in person. This not only makes you more of a "person" to the opposing party, but it shows them that you value the relationship and are showing up to have the hard talk.

- If you cannot be there in person, be there on their screen. Facetime or Skype them. Videoconference if needed. At the very least, have the phone conversation. Avoid text and writing at all costs and resort to it only when necessary. And finally, do not use social media to disagree with someone. It may be tempting, but it is futile. It is not effective and typically a waste of time.

Conclusion

"At the end of reasons comes persuasion."

-Ludwig Wittgenstein

Thank you for making it through to the end of *Persuasion: The Complete Psychologist's Guide to Highly Effective Persuasion and Manipulation Techniques – Influence People with NLP, Mind Control and Human Behavior Psychology*. Let's hope it was informative and able to provide you with all of the tools you need to achieve your goals.

The next step is to start practicing the skills in this book. Seek out people you do not know to hone your small talk talents. Mentally prepare yourself to sit and listen to what people have to say. Look to disarm disagreements with kindness and understanding. Persuade people to follow your lead with natural grace and poise. Using the techniques and suggestions in this book, you can successfully control people's thoughts and get them to do what you want. Just remember, this power can be used for good or bad reasons. The more influence and persuasion you control over others, the more this responsibility is important. Remain persuasive to the betterment of those around you, and you will not be at a shortage of authority or power.

A successful application of persuasion does not mean you will always experience this win. This also means that a failed attempt does not mean you are never going to enjoy the ability to get people to follow your way of thinking. This is a process and requires training. You must practice to get better and better. The more you communicate with others, the more opportunity you will get to become the persuasive leader you seek to be. Apply this persuasion in your home, with friends, family, or at work. When you are guiding and communicating naturally, you will experience the power of persuasion that has been a part of human nature since the beginning.

Part of this process is to be aware and observant of yourself and others. You must understand what persuasion is, the reason you are seeking to influence another person or group of people, and how you will present yourself and your argument in a manner that gets people to want to listen and follow-up. Of course, there will be those who are resistant or do not want to be persuaded. This just means you get to put those skills to the test and challenge your powers of persuasion. Use the final chapter of this book to remind you how best to deal with those who conflict or disagree with you, or who just plain refuse to listen to what you have to say. With time, patience, and practice you will be able to control your mind and those of others in any situation.

Emotional Intelligence

The Complete Psychologist's Guide to Mastering Social Skills, Improve Your Relationships, Boost Your EQ and Self Mastery

Introduction

I bet if you were asked two decades ago what are the factors that determine a person's overall success in life, you would have said: a high intelligence quotient, good grades, and well-developed cognitive functions. It was natural to assume that people with high intelligence in general had higher chances of being successful. Parents, educators, and peers sang the same tune of high intelligence translating into greater success. We wish it was actually that simple!

If you want to be successful in life, you need to study hard, get awesome grades, go to college, study harder, and graduate with really high honors. This path was believed to be the guaranteed shot to a great job and an abundantly successful life.

You spent years believing this notion, and though it's not completely incorrect, it's not the full picture either. Success is the result of a combination of various factors, and the most fundamental of them is your ability to handle your own and other people's emotions.

Emotional intelligence, or emotional quotient, (both represent the same idea), is a type of intelligence that refers to an individual's ability to recognize and manage or control their own and other people's emotions. It is a simple and straightforward concept that comprises two main components:

- Identifying or recognizing emotions, intentions, desires, and goals in yourself and other people.

- Managing these emotions and actions to accomplish the most positive outcome for everyone involved.

Research on emotional intelligence has been ongoing since the mid-20th century within the psycho-scientific community. However, it wasn't until 1995, when Daniel Goleman published his book by the same name, that emotional intelligence rolled into the mainstream consciousness and became a ground-breaking concept. Back then, intelligence quotient was seen as the only factor that mattered when it came to assessing an individual's capabilities. Once emotional intelligence took over, IQ was perceived as a narrow or limited way of assessing an individual's chances of success. The cut-throat world of career, jobs, and business was starkly different from the cushy confines of a classroom.

If one had to navigate the real world, they'd have to adapt to a different kind of intelligence than the academic one used in classrooms or libraries. A person's knowledge and cognitive abilities alone didn't guarantee success in life. A degree didn't automatically mean a high paying job or a profitable business.

At best, you'll get your foot through the door. However, for someone to succeed, you would need much more than just plain intelligence. It would take social, communication, conversation, and emotional skills to raise the bar. These are life skills that don't come in the classroom but are learned by living in a hostel, waiting at bars, joining social clubs, being a part of sports teams, and volunteering.

Do you still think IQ is the only factor that determines a person's overall success in life? If that was true, my friend, every successful person you spot today from the CEO of big organizations to the president, to thought leaders, and successful entrepreneurs should be a Harvard, Stanford, MIT graduate with a Ph.D.

Make a list of ten successful people you admire the most. They are the people you look up to as they lead successful and balanced lives. Are all these folks top honors graduates from distinguished educational institutions with a high IQ? My money is on 'No!'

Again, don't get me wrong here. I am not undermining the importance of intelligence or asking you to shut that book on mechanical engineering and start reading about human psychology. It is awesome if you possess naturally high cognitive abilities and a high intelligence quotient. All I am saying is, you should ideally have both EQ and IQ complementing each other to increase your chances of success in the real world.

If you can increase your emotional quotient to back up an already high intelligence quotient, you can achieve many great things!

However, if you ask me to pick between two skills, I would have to go with emotional intelligence. A person with average intelligence and highly evolved emotional intelligence has a greater chance of succeeding in today's world than a person with high intelligence and less developed emotional intelligence. The name of the game today is about managing people, understanding their emotions or motives, and managing their feelings to achieve the most positive results.

Technical knowledge may help you direct or instruct your team when it comes to completing a task. However, your ability to keep them motivated by understanding their emotions will ensure they'll stay inspired and productive throughout the process.

A person's cognitive intelligence or intellectual potential has always been measured as his or her ability to retain facts or make calculations. However, these skills aren't necessarily all-encompassing in certain positions such as leadership and entrepreneurship. Tons of CEOs, world leaders, and Fortune 500 company founders are high-school dropouts. If intelligence alone was the measure of a person's success, how would you explain this?

The reality is that it isn't as straightforward as a single factor like intelligence that determines our success. It is, in fact, a combination of factors which are mainly emotional and social life skills that will help you survive or thrive in the real world. Intelligence quotient is an inborn, but not all-inclusive, factor that can influence an individual's success in life.

This is good news because, irrespective of your traditional, genetically determined intelligence, you have a good chance of being successful if you work on other social-emotional life skills. A high emotional quotient along with other social and psychological skill sets can definitely boost your chances.

The objective of this book is to discuss crucial aspects of emotional intelligence and how to use them in your everyday life to make your dream of being successful a reality. We'll take a look at practical techniques to raise your emotional quotient and eventually boost your chances of success.

Chapter 1: History of Emotional Intelligence Models

Harry and Pete both have a heated argument with their boss. Once Harry gets home, he starts yelling at his children for making noise and not going to bed. On the other hand, Pete doesn't yell or scream at his children even though they are making noise and not in bed yet.

While Harry chides his children rudely for making a mess with their toys, Pete gently, yet assertively, urges them to put their toys in their place and get ready to sleep. Harry doesn't know how to handle his negative emotions that are a direct result of his argument with the boss. He invariably ends up directing that anger towards his children, who aren't connected to the argument in any manner.

Pete understands that he is upset with his boss and not his children. Therefore, there is no point in screaming at his children. It will only make things worse for him.

In the above scenario, both Harry and Pete faced the same emotions, yet the manner in which they expressed a similar emotion differed drastically. Pete was able to identify and manage his emotions differently than Harry, who allowed his emotions to get the better of him.

This is the essence of emotional intelligence. Being able to recognize your own and other people's emotions and the ability to manage these emotions effectively to create a positive and pleasant outcome.

Essentially, emotional intelligence (EQ) is the knack of perceiving, managing, and evaluating emotions to create the desired positive outcome. The term was made popular by Daniel Goleman in 1995 with his ground-breaking book of the same name. However, emotional intelligence as a term was first used by Michael Beldoch in the mid-20th century.

It is the ability to monitor not just your own, but also other people's feelings, distinguish between emotions, label feelings, and leverage this emotional information to direct your thoughts and actions. This is a broader and more general definition of emotional intelligence, though there are differences within the scientific community about what it encompasses. The unanimous view is that it is a skill that involves identifying, understanding, and managing emotions.

Emotional intelligence ability model

The emotional intelligence model was created by Mayer and Salovey, who defined emotional quotient as the ability to correctly recognize, evaluate, and generate emotions to facilitate thought, gain a better understanding of emotions, and manage emotions for enhancing both cognitive and emotional development.

The psychologist duo believed that an individual must be assessed on four distinct interconnected abilities to determine their overall EQ. The four abilities are:

- **Recognizing emotions**

This involves picking up verbal and non-verbal clues for understanding a person's emotions.

- **Reasoning or using these emotions to facilitate thinking and intellectual activity**

For example, leveraging emotions to offer solutions or reviewing situations. This helps us focus our limited attention span on the right things and react as per the situation. This benefits the overall creative process.

- **Understanding emotions**

Human emotions are complex. They hold multiple meanings and guide us in understanding another person's emotional state of mind. They help us understand other people's emotions and why people feel the way they do. Emotions have several nuances and aren't often as straightforward as they appear. Every emotion holds its own pattern of thoughts, actions, and intentions.

For example, if a person is hurt, you will be able to deduce why he or she feels hurt. An individual with this particular ability can immediately understand another person's emotional state and why they are thinking or behaving in a certain manner.

- **Regulating emotions**

  This is the ability to manage your own and other people's emotions by responding suitably to them. For instance, you know how to react appropriately when a person is angry or upset. In the example at the beginning of the chapter, we saw how Pete was able to regulate his emotions positively, even though both he and Harry experienced similar emotions. Controlling our own and other people's emotions is a major component of emotional intelligence.

Salovey-Mayer concluded that an individual may be closed to emotional signals that are too painful or uncomfortable while being open to those that aren't overwhelming. This is calculated through the Mayer-Salovey-Caruso Emotional Intelligence Test (MESCEIT). It is measured by emotion-focused problem-solving.

Mixed model emotional intelligence

This model of emotional intelligence was founded on Daniel Goleman's 25 distinct emotional intelligence traits, which encompasses everything from teamwork, service orientation, and accomplishment motivation to self-awareness.

It is referred to as a mixed model since it merges emotional intelligence traits with other personality characteristics that are linked neither with emotion nor intelligence. Emotional competence is a capability that can be learned and developed to create outstanding results. This emotional intelligence model is based on five primary categories, each one with clear emotional competencies:

- **Self-awareness**

  Self-awareness is the ability to identify an emotion as we experience it. We tune in to our inner selves for assessing what exactly we are feeling and how to best regulate it. Self-awareness comprises self-confidence in your capabilities and emotional awareness in realizing what you are feeling and the subsequent emotional effects.

- **Self-regulation**

  We think we don't have great control over our emotions, but negative emotions can be managed through various self-regulating techniques like walking, prayer, running, and meditation. To self-regulate effectively, one needs to have control over their impulsive actions, must demonstrate honesty and integrity, possess creative thinking, must be able to handle change easily, and can take responsibility for their actions.

- **Motivation**

Motivation is the ability to work towards fulfilling a set of goals. The most important aspect of this category is positive thinking. To become a positive thinker, one must always stay positive and be capable of restructuring negative thoughts. This can be accomplished by optimism, commitment, initiative, and drive for achievement. You are perpetually involved in the pursuit of improving yourself to become a better person.

- **Empathy**

Empathy is a huge component of emotional intelligence. It is the ability to not just discern people's emotions but also to 'feel' what they feel. Empathy is about understanding others, being able to anticipate other people's needs, helping others develop their qualities, and building relationships with people who are quite different from you. Empathy is comprised of more than a single ability. However, fundamentally, it is about being able to feel and relate to other people's emotions.

- **Social skills**
  Relating to other people is another important attribute of emotional intelligence. Social skills are important in teamwork, collaboration, communication, influence, building relationships, and conflict management.

This emotional quotient model measures emotional intelligence with the 'Emotional Competence Inventory' and 'Emotional Intelligence Appraisal.'

Emotional intelligence trait model

The trait type emotional intelligence model was developed by Petrides (and his co-workers) in 2009 to assess emotional quotient. It shifts from the previous ability-based model and talks about how people possess specific emotional characteristics or traits and self-perceptions based on their unique personality.

Basically, emotional intelligence is an individual's self-perceptions about their emotional capabilities, behavior, actions, and abilities. Another label for the same concept is emotional self-efficiency. These traits aren't assessed in the real scientific way. Rather, they are analyzed by a respondent's self-analysis. The 'Trait Emotional Questionnaire' measures an individual's ability to accurately list their own traits.

Brief history of emotional intelligence

The term 'emotional intelligence' was first coined by Peter Salovey and John D. Mayer in 1990, describing it as a type of social intelligence involving the ability to regulate one's own emotions as well as other people's feelings and emotions, to differentiate among these emotions, and to utilize this information for guiding one's thoughts and actions.

Salovey and Mayer launched a research program for measuring a person's emotional intelligence and exploring its significance. For example, there was a study conducted on a group of people, where it was discovered that people who can identify and give a clear name to emotions were able to recover easily from an upsetting film they'd watched.

In another experiment, people who scored high in their ability to perceive things correctly and identify or understand other people's emotions were able to respond more effectively to changes within their social circle and build social support networks.

During the early 90s, Daniel Goleman became acquainted with Salovey and Mayer's research, which led him to author *Emotional Intelligence*. Goleman's school of emotional intelligence believed that it wasn't cognitive intelligence that guaranteed a person's business success, but a person's ability to manage his own and other people's emotions that determined his chances of success. He stated that emotionally intelligent people possess four primary characteristics:

1. People with high emotional intelligence are good at identifying their emotions or have good self-awareness.
2. They mastered the ability to manage their emotions.
3. They were able to show empathy to the emotions of other people.
4. They were efficient at handling other's emotions.

The seeds of emotional intelligence were sown way back in the 1930s when the concept of 'social intelligence' was put forth by Edward Thorndike. He described it as the ability to form interpersonal and social relationships with people.

In the 1940s, David Wechsler suggested that attributes of effective intelligence may be responsible for success.

During the 1950s, humanistic psychologist Abraham Maslow described how people can develop emotional strength.

In 1953, people started thinking about emotions and intelligence. Dorothy Van Ghent described how novels such as Jane Austen's *Pride and Prejudice* featured characters with high emotional intelligence.

In 1975, Howard Gardner published *The Shattered Mind*, which discussed the concept of different types of intelligence apart from cognitive intelligence.

In 1987, *Mensa Magazine* published an article in which Keith Beasley uses "emotional quotient" as a phrase for the first time. This was the first published use of the term, though Reuven Bar-on claimed to use the term in his unpublished thesis prior to the Mensa article.

In 1990, Peter Salovey and John Meyer's groundbreaking article on emotional intelligence is published.

In 1995, the concept of Emotional Intelligence is made popular all over the world after *New York Times* writer Daniel Goleman's publication of *Emotional Intelligence: Why It Can Matter More Than IQ.* Goleman drew from Salovey and Meyer's research to talk about emotional intelligence as a vital type of intelligence for success in academics and work.

One of the most crucial aspects of emotional intelligence is that, unlike intelligence quotient, emotional intelligence is not fixed. While some people are born with an aptitude for various emotional and social components, emotional intelligence is largely malleable.

Emotional intelligence experts agree that conventional intelligence contributes to a mere 10-25 percent of our success. A major chunk of it, however, is determined by multiple factors, including our ability to manage our own and other people's emotions.

Research conducted by Harvard graduates across several professions, including medicine and law, concluded there was a zero and, at times, a negative correlation between high entrance test scores and success in various professions. This clearly establishes that a high intelligence quotient, or knowledge, alone doesn't determine a person's chances of succeeding.

Research headed by Dr. Travis Bradberry concluded that 90 percent of top performing workers in an organization possess high emotional intelligence. People with high emotional quotient also earn $29,000 more annually than their counterparts with low emotional intelligence within the same profession. Thus, people with high emotional intelligence are not only more productive and efficient but also, on an average, make more money than people with low emotional intelligence.

Goleman's emotional intelligence framework

Goleman's emotional intelligence framework focuses on the idea that emotional quotient, or intelligence, is an important factor in personal, professional, and social success. The framework states that emotional quotient has five fundamental domains which are then divided into four separate quadrants. A couple of these domains are linked to personal abilities, while the remaining two are linked with social competencies.

Goleman's theory is popular worldwide because it speaks of emotional intelligence as an ability that can be developed in contrast to intelligence quotient, which is largely predetermined by genetic factors.

While personal competencies are categorized into self-awareness and self-management, social competencies are divided into social awareness and relationship management. Self-awareness is the ability to identify your own emotions and their impact on yourself and others around you. Self-regulation, or management, is about managing or regulating your emotions to ensure emotions don't end up controlling you.

Social awareness includes organizational awareness, service orientation, and empathy. Relationship management includes leadership, inspiring and developing others, influence, change catalyst, building connections, teamwork, communication, and collaboration.

Self-awareness
Self-awareness is the ability to recognize one's feelings and their consequences. People with high self-awareness possess the following competencies:

- They know the emotions they are experiencing and why they are experiencing these emotions.

- They recognize how their emotions impact their performance.

- They are aware of their strengths and limitations.

- Self-aware people are open to constructive criticism or feedback, fresher perspectives, constant learning, and personal development.

- They are decisive by nature and can make clear decisions even when they're under stress and faced with uncertainties.

- People with high self-awareness are able to establish the connection between people's feelings, thoughts, and actions.

- They are able to display a sense a of humor and view themselves from a lighter perspective. People who indulge in self-deprecating humor are often confident, self-assured, and emotionally intelligent people.

- People with high self-awareness do not feel the need to go with the tide. They are happy to stand alone and voice views that do not match popular views.

Self-regulation

Self-regulation is the ability to manage disturbing emotions and emotional impulses that can hinder interpersonal relationships and performance. Here are some competencies that people with high self-regulation possess:

- People with high emotional self-control can manage their impulses and disturbing emotions effectively.

- They are able to stay calm, positive, and unaffected even in the most trying circumstances.

- People with high self-regulation are able to build trust and credibility through reliability, integrity, and authenticity. They are also able to accept their own mistakes and are brave enough to call out others for their unethical acts.

- High self-regulation abilities lead these people to meet commitments, keep promises, and act on their word.

- They are also highly effective in handling change and adapting to new scenarios.

Social awareness
Social awareness is understanding other people's feelings and views and taking a keen interest in their concerns as if it is one's own concern. People who have high empathy possess the following abilities:

- They are extremely perceptive to verbal and nonverbal emotional clues while listening to people.

- They show understanding for another person's point of view even though they may not necessarily agree with it.

- They are happy to help solve people's problems and concerns in any manner within their capacity.

- People with high social awareness acknowledge other people's accomplishments and reward them for their strengths.

Social skills
Social skills are the ability to influence and persuade people. People with high social skills possess the following competencies:

- They are able to deal with conflicts in an assertive and straightforward manner.

- They practice open communication and are receptive to both praise and criticism.

- People with high social skills can inspire others to pursue a shared goal or vision.

Impact of emotional intelligence in daily life — examples
Let us say you've been offered constructive feedback by your manager about areas you can improve upon or areas where you didn't perform to your fullest potential. People with a low emotional quotient may take the criticism personally or come up with a host of excuses and blame games to cover their shortcomings. They may not accept their mistakes or they may find a scapegoat to blame their inefficacy on. They may get angry, irritable, depressed, and demotivated. Acting on emotions is easier. Identifying them and regulating them takes work.

Conversely, an individual with greater emotional intelligence will accept the fact that no one is perfect. Rather than taking the feedback personally, they'll introspect about what their manager said and work on areas of improvement to become more efficient. They will stop making similar mistakes. People with a high emotional quotient will actively seek feedback from others rather than focus on proving themselves right. They are less likely to argue and blame others for their shortcomings.

Emotionally intelligent people are open to suggestions and constructive feedback, which eventually helps them accomplish their objectives. For these folks, being right is being more efficient. They value feedback and actively work on it. This is just one of the ways high emotional intelligence can positively affect your productivity and success in the workplace.

Let us now take another example in a personal scenario.

You are involved in a heated discussion about political ideologies with your best friend. While your friend is fervently putting forth their views about their ideology, you firmly stick to your opinion. When they speak, they appear angry. An emotionally intelligent person can quickly gauge this emotion and understand the impact of the topic on their friend. You realize that you could end up hurting or upsetting them if the topic continues for a while.

A person with high emotional intelligence gets a grip on the circumstances easily and gently acknowledges the other person's view even if they don't necessarily subscribe to those ideas. They may not agree with their friend, but they are accepting their right to disagree. Since this person is more thoughtful, empathetic, and sensitive to other people's needs, they can successfully stop a discussion from blowing into a full-fledged fight. Thus, things finish on a constructive and positive note.

Now, consider the same scenario with a person who isn't emotionally intelligent or empathetic towards other people's feelings. This kind of person is adamantly focused on their views. They refuse to understand where the other person is coming from. Thus, the discussion snowballs into a heated argument. They fan the flame of the difference even more. The results are anger, hurt, and negativity. The fight ends badly and affects their interpersonal relationship.

We can all identify that one emotionally intelligent person within our family, friends, or social circle. They always say the most appropriate thing to say in any situation. They can pacify people, thwart potentially uncomfortable situations, nip arguments in the bud, and arrive at a solution where everyone is pleased. Irrespective of how tricky a scenario is, they manage to find their way through it by using emotional information about their own and other people's feelings.

They excel in handling challenging situations that involve differences between people and know how to assert themselves without offending anyone. These are the empathetic, considerate, and caring folks who also know how to assert themselves. Any wonder that most companies today demand people with high emotional intelligence for filling leadership positions?

While people with a high intelligence quotient may have the answer or solution to your problems, emotionally intelligent people can make you feel more hopeful about the situation.

Chapter 2: Solid Tips for Boosting Emotional Self-awareness

The first step towards developing greater emotional intelligence is boosting self-awareness, or your understanding of your own feelings and emotions. You can regulate your emotions for an optimally positive outcome only if you are able to identify these emotions. Labeling emotions and determining your actions based on these emotions is critical to the process of developing emotional intelligence. When you are more aware of your feelings and emotions, recognizing other people's emotions becomes simpler.

Here are solid, proven tips for boosting self-awareness to get you started on the path of emotional intelligence:

Label your emotions
Label and categorize your emotions. I know this makes your feelings sound like they belong to a library. However, labeling, or giving names to your emotions, makes it easier to identify and act upon them. When you feel an emotion surging through you, attempt to identify it quickly. Is it fear, insecurity, jealousy, anger, elation, depression, surprise, or a combination of these emotions?

Identify the triggers that cause these emotions. For instance, a specific person may evoke jealousy in you because you feel they are more successful than you.

What makes you feel certain emotions? What are the triggers that anger or hurt you? What makes you happy and sad? What is the source of positive and destructive emotions in you? Labeling your feelings and recognizing the stimuli for various emotions will increase your emotional self-awareness.

Grab a pen and paper to list your emotions when you experience a compelling feeling. Mention the precise emotion or feeling that you are experiencing. Accompany this emotional label with the trigger that caused it. What is it that made you feel the way you do? When you recognize an emotion, it is easier to manage it.

For instance, let us assume you feel a deep sense of loathing for a person without any specific reason. You dislike them and can't stand them, but funnily, can't tell why you dislike them. Upon closer examination of your feelings, you realize you dislike them because you are envious of them. You may believe they are always having a wonderful life, while things never go your way. By nailing this emotion as jealousy, you can regulate your potentially negative emotions.

Once you recognize the emotion as irrational jealousy, you will view it in a more logical and understanding manner. You'll begin to think along the lines that it isn't really someone's fault that they lead an amazing life. In fact, they should be applauded for working hard towards their goals. You'll realize that no one has a perfect life. Everyone goes through shares of trials and tribulation to attain success, which isn't necessarily visible to the outside world. Sometimes, it is only how we perceive things and not the reality. Thus, once you are more mindful of your emotions, you can work with them more positively.

Be an expert on yourself
What is the one thing you should do to bring about changes in your thoughts, actions, and behavior? The answer is: awareness about these thoughts and subsequent actions! To make changes, you ought to know what you have to improve upon.

Knowing yourself inside out is the key to being more emotionally aware and savvy. Did you know athletes are trained to identify and overcome feelings before an important upcoming game? This is based on the premise that if you can successfully identify and control your emotions, it doesn't impact your productivity.

Go back and think about all the recent instances where you let emotions get the better of you and affect your productivity. Haven't you let trivial matters impact your performance?

By being aware of your strengths and weaknesses, it is easier to confidently accomplish your objectives. There is a lesser scope for frustration, low productivity, and disappointment. Self-confidence increases your assertiveness while you express your thoughts and opinions, which is important for developing social skills.

Once you gain greater awareness, you will rarely be ruled by emotions. You have a clear edge if you are able to regulate your emotions. An emotionally aware person stops being a victim of his emotions and uses these emotions in a positive way to reach a desired outcome.

Spend time recognizing areas of development to strengthen them

- List all your strengths and weaknesses.

- Take a formal, psychological personality assessment test that helps you discover your own skills, abilities, limitations, and values.

- Obtain objective feedback from people you trust.

One way that works wonders for increasing your self-awareness is journaling. Write in a flowing stream of consciousness about the thoughts you are feeling and experiencing as they are occurring. What are the emotions you are experiencing? What are the physiological reactions to your feelings?

Are you experiencing a faster heartbeat, sweaty palms, increased pulse, etc. as a physical reaction to your emotions?

Emotions aren't always straightforward. In fact, they are complex and multi-layered. For example, you may have a heated argument with your partner and feel angry, hurt, upset, and vengeful all at the same time. Write emotions exactly as you are experiencing them, even if two emotions appear to contradict each other. For instance, if you've got a scholarship to study overseas, you may be elated at the opportunity. However, the thought of leaving behind your partner may cause a twinge of sadness, too. You are acknowledging and validating your emotions by writing them.

Dexter Valles, the CEO of Valmar International, suggests carrying a whiteboard divided into two to three parts throughout the day. Add six to eight feelings to the board and ask employees to put a check on the feelings they experience at different points during the day. Determine which emotions have the maximum check marks.

Make a list of every role you play in your daily life such as being a parent, sibling, volunteer, worker, and more. What are the emotions linked with each role? For example, you may enjoy your role as a parent, but you can also be an unhappy employee. Examine every role and the emotions attached to it carefully.

Naming emotions linked to every relationship will help you manage emotions within that relationship more efficiently. It will keep you in greater control of your emotional reaction where the specific role is concerned.

Do a frequent check-in
Do a frequent check-in with your emotions much like how you have a waiter checking in with you frequently to know if you need anything. You do a mental check-in of your emotions periodically to understand how you are feeling at different times during the day. It is a sort of, "Hello, mind, how are you feeling? What can be done to make you feel better?"

Examine the origin of these specific feelings. Are you feeling low and deflated because your boss said something to you in the morning? Are you feeling angry and hurt because you fought with your partner? Are you experiencing certain physiological symptoms as a result of these emotions or feelings? Are these emotions impacting your body language, posture, gestures, and expressions? Are these emotions evident or visible to others? Are you more transparent when it comes to expressing your emotions? Are your decisions primarily determined by emotions?

If you want to be a more emotionally balanced person, reconnect with your primary emotions, recognize them, accept the emotions, and use them for making better decisions.

Use third person

Research in the field of labeling our emotions has indicated that when we distance ourselves from our emotions, or view them more objectively, we gain higher self-awareness. Next time you feel the urge to say, "I am disappointed," try to say, "Jack is disappointed."

If that seems too preposterous, try saying, "I am presently experiencing sadness," or, "One of my feelings at the moment is sadness."

These are techniques through which you are distancing yourself from overpowering emotions to stay naturally composed. You are basically treating your emotions as just another piece of information rather than being overwhelmed by them.

Each time you find yourself experiencing an urge to react to a situation, take a moment to name it. Then use it in the third person to distance yourself from intense emotions.

Emotions don't always need to be fixed

You don't always have to identify emotions with the intention of fixing them. Self-awareness is not about fixing emotions. It is about recognizing these emotions and letting them pass rather than allowing them to get the better of you. Society has conditioned us to think that certain emotions are bad. We mistakenly believe that experiencing these emotions makes us a bad person.

Far from it, emotions aren't good or bad. They are just that, emotions. There's no need to push away the seemingly bad emotions. Acknowledge that you are experiencing an emotion by saying something like, "I am experiencing jealousy." Practice deep breathing for a while until the emotion passes. Rather than pushing the emotion away and, in the process, increasing its intensity to come back even stronger, gently acknowledge it and let it be until it passes.

It takes around six seconds for the body to absorb chemicals that can alter your emotions. Give your body that much time.

We often share a hostile relationship with our emotions. They are believed to be something that is negative and should be fought or suppressed. However, emotions are information that helps us function in our daily lives. Overcome the mindset that emotions are good or bad, and instead focus on using them to empower you. Rather than letting emotions take control of you, use emotional information to work with them.

Emotions are neural hormones that are released as a direct response to our perceptions regarding the world. They direct us towards a specific action. All emotions have a distinct message and objective, which means there's no such thing as a good or bad emotion.

For example, fear helps us focus on an impending danger and take the necessary action to defend ourselves. Similarly, sadness makes us experience a sense of loss and facilitates a better understanding of what we truly care about.

If you move away from your best friend and become sad, this mean you truly care about them so much that you experienced sadness. This is valuable information. Hence, sadness is not a bad emotion. It can be used to identify what you care about.

If you use emotions as information for recognizing feelings, they can be channeled positively. The number one rule for developing higher emotional intelligence is to stop judging and curbing your emotions.

Train yourself to identify emotions based on physiological reactions

Our emotions often have physical manifestations. For example, you may feel anxious before a job interview or an important presentation. You experience the sensation of having 'butterflies in your stomach' before addressing an audience on the stage.

Don't you find your heart pounding with excitement when you are about to go on a date with someone you've fancied for long? Nervousness leaves us with sweaty palms and stiff muscles.

While these are only some of the physiological reactions we experience with our emotions, research has proven that a variety of emotions are strongly associated with stimulating certain parts of the body.

Regular patterns of physical sensations are linked with each of the six fundamental emotions, including fear, happiness, anger, sadness, disgust, and surprise. Human emotions discreetly overlap physiological sensations. For example, lower limb sensations are associated with sadness. Similarly, increased upper limb sensations are connected with anger. A strong feeling of disgust generates sensations within the throat and digestive system. Fear and surprise generate sensations in the chest.

Identify recurring patterns
This can be one of the most effective parts of knowing yourself. Neuroscience will help you understand the process more effectively. Our brains have an inherent tendency to follow established neural paths rather than creating new ones. This doesn't necessarily mean that the established patterns are serving us positively or that they can't be altered.

For instance, when a person becomes angry, he or she may bottle up their emotion rather than express it. This has become an emotional pattern with the person and is deeply embedded in the mind. However, awareness of this pattern can help the person chart another course of action, where the person practices responding instead of simply reacting to the emotion. However, the first step to charting a new pattern is identifying a pattern.

Recognize the build-up of emotions before something suddenly triggers you. These triggers have a predictable pattern. If you are already frustrated, you are more likely to see a situation in a more negative light. Similarly, if you are overcome by fear, you are more likely to interpret a stimulus as a threat. It is therefore important to be aware of these biases and how they can impact our emotions by creating a predictable pattern. The more efficient you become in recognizing your biases, the lower your chances of misinterpreting a stimulus.

Work with what you know about emotions
Emotions are important pieces of data that help you gauge things from a clearer and objective perspective. Don't suppress, ignore, fight, or feel overwhelmed by your emotions. Instead, you should build a valuable library of experiences with them. The purpose of emotional awareness is to concentrate our attention on these emotions and use them positively to create the desired outcome.

Treat your emotions as data that relies on your view of the world, or as a guide on how to act. When you open yourself to this data, you enjoy access to a huge resource of emotions that can be utilized to drive your actions in the right direction. You will know exactly how to reach wherever it is that you want to go if you have a clear emotional route. Therefore, you should acknowledge and recognize your emotions as data, and work with them instead of trying to beat them.

Begin by carefully noticing how you feel at the moment. Observe emotions without judging them or attempting to fix them. Learn to simply notice your emotions.

Be receptive to feedback and constructive criticism

One of the best ways to develop greater awareness of your emotions is to be more open to feedback and criticism from others. For instance, a friend may tell you that each time they talk about their accomplishments they sense your pangs of envy or dislike towards them. This may help you tune into your emotions and emotional triggers more effectively.

Emotionally intelligent folks are open to receiving feedback, and they always consider the other person's point of view. You may not necessarily agree with them, but listening to other people's criticism and feedback helps you work on your blind spots. This can help you recognize your thoughts, triggers, and behavioral patterns.

I know a person who, in a bid to increase his self-awareness and emotional quotient, actively goes around asking people for feedback about his words, feelings (as they understand it), and actions. It acts as an emotion meter, which helps him gain greater awareness of his emotions and regulate them more efficiently.

Chapter 3: Emotional Intelligence and Delaying Gratification

I am guessing you do know about the famous 'marshmallow test' of emotional intelligence. If you don't, here it is:

During the 1960s, social psychologist Walter Mischel headed several psychological studies on delayed rewards and gratification. He closely studied hundreds of children between the ages of 4 to 5 years to reveal a trait that is known to be one of the most important factors that determine success in a person's life, gratification.

This experiment is famously referred to as the marshmallow test. The experiment involved introducing every child into a private chamber and placing a single marshmallow in front of them. At this stage, the researcher struck a deal with the child.

The researcher informed them that he would be gone from the chamber for a while. The child was then informed that if he or she didn't eat the marshmallow while the researcher was away, he would come back and reward them with an additional marshmallow apart from the one on the table. However, if they did eat the marshmallow placed on the table in front of them, they wouldn't be rewarded with another.

It was clear. One marshmallow immediately or two marshmallows later.

The researcher walked out of the chamber and re-entered after 15 minutes.

Predictably, some children leaped on the marshmallow in front of them and ate it as soon as the researcher walked out of the room. However, others tried hard to restrain themselves by diverting their attention. They bounced, jumped around, and scooted on the chairs to distract themselves in a bid to stop themselves from eating the marshmallow. However, many of these children failed to resist the temptation and eventually gave in.

Only a handful of children managed to hold until the very end without eating the marshmallow.

The study was published in 1972 and became globally popular as 'The Marshmallow Experiment.' However, it doesn't end here. The real twist in the tale is what followed several years later.

Researchers undertook a follow-up study to track the life and progress of each child who was a part of the initial experiment. They studied several areas of the person's life and were surprised by what they discovered. The children who delayed gratification for higher rewards or waited until the end to earn two marshmallows instead of one had higher school grades, lower instances of substance abuse, lower chances of obesity, and better stress coping abilities.

The research was known as a ground-breaking study on gratification because researchers followed up on the children 40 years after the initial experiment was conducted, and it was sufficiently evident that the group of children who delayed gratification patiently for higher rewards succeeded in all areas they were measured on.

This experiment proved beyond doubt that delaying gratification is one of the most crucial skills for success in life.

Success and delaying gratification
Success usually boils down to picking between the discomfort of discipline over the pleasure or comfort of distraction. This is exactly what delaying gratification is. Would you rather go out for the new movie in town where all your friends are heading, or would you rather sit up and study for an examination to earn good grades? Would you rather party hard with your co-workers before the team gets started with an important upcoming presentation? Or would you sit late and work on fine tuning the presentation?

Our ability to delay gratification is also a huge factor when it comes to decision making and is considered an important aspect of emotional intelligence. Each day, we make several choices and decisions. While some are trivial and have little influence on our future (what color shoes should I buy? Or which way should I take to work?), others have a huge bearing on our success and future.

As human beings, we are wired to make decisions or choices that offer an instant return on investment. We want quick results, actions, and rewards. The mind is naturally tuned for a short-term profit. Why do you think e-commerce giants are making a killing by charging an additional fee for same day and next day delivery? Today is better than tomorrow!

Think about how different our life would be if we thought about the impact of our decisions about three to five years from now? If we can bring about this mental shift where we can delay gratification by keeping our eyes firmly fixated on the bigger picture several years from now, our lives can be very different.

Another factor that is important in gratification delay is the environment. For example, if children who were able to resist temptation were not given a second marshmallow or reward for delaying gratification, they are less likely to view delaying gratification as a positive habit.

If parents do not keep their commitment to reward a child for delaying gratification, the child won't value the trait. Delaying gratification can be picked up only in an environment of commitment and trust, where a second marshmallow is given when deserved.

Examples of gratification delay

Let us say you want to buy your dream car that you see in the showroom on your way to work every day. You imagine how wonderful it would be to own and drive that car. The car costs $25,000, and you barely have $5000 dollars in your current savings. How do you buy the car then? Simple, you start saving. This is how you will combine strong willpower with delayed gratification.

There are countless opportunities for you to blow money every day such as hitting the bar with friends for a drink on weekends, co-workers visiting the nearest coffee shop to grab a latte, or buying expensive gadgets. Every time you remove your wallet to pay, you have two clear choices: either blow your money on monetary pleasure or wait for the long-term reward. If you can resist these temptations and curtail your expenses, you'll be closer to purchasing your dream car. Making this decision will help you buy a highly desirable thing in future.

Will you spend now for immediate gratifications and pleasures, or will you save to buy something more valuable in the future?

Here is another interesting example to elucidate the concept of delayed gratification. Let us say you want to be the best film director the world has ever seen. You want to master the craft and pick up all skills related to movie making and the entertainment business. You visualize yourself as making spectacular movies that inspire and entertain people for decades.

How do you plan to work towards a large goal, or the big picture (well, literally)? You'll start by doing mundane, boring, uninspiring jobs on the sets such as being someone's assistant, fetching them a cup of coffee, cleaning the sets, and other similar boring chores. It isn't exciting or fun, but you go through it each day because you have your eyes firmly fixated on the larger goal, or bigger picture.

You know you want to become a huge filmmaker one day and are prepared to delay gratification for fulfilling that goal. The discomfort of your current life is smaller in comparison to the pleasure of the higher goal. This is delayed gratification. Despite the discomfort, you regulate your actions and behavior for meeting a bigger goal in the future. It may be tough and boring currently, but you know that doing these arduous tasks will give you that shot to make it big someday.

Delayed gratification can be applicable in all aspects of life from health to relationships. Almost every decision we make involves a decision between opting for short-term pleasures now and enjoying bigger rewards later. A burger can give you immediate pleasure today, whereas an apple may not give you instant pleasure but will benefit your body in the long run.

Stop drop technique

Each time you identify an overpowering or stressful emotion that is compelling you to seek immediate pleasure, describe your feelings by writing them down. Make sure you state them clearly to acknowledge their existence.

Have you seen the old VCR models? They had a big pause button prominently placed in the middle. You are now going to push the pause button on your thoughts.

Focus all attention on the heart as it is the center of all your feelings.

Think of something remarkably beautiful that you experienced. It can be a spectacular sunset you witnessed on one of your trips, a beautiful flower you saw in a garden today, or a cute pet kitten you spotted in the neighborhood. Basically, anything that evokes feelings of joy, happiness, and positivity in you. The idea is to bring about a shift in your feelings.

Experience the feeling for some time and allow it to linger. Imagine the feelings you experience in and around your heart. If it is still challenging, take deep breaths. Hold the positive feeling and enjoy it.

Now, click on the mental pause button and revisit the compelling idea that was causing stressful feelings. How does it feel right now?

Now write down how you are feeling and what comes to mind. Act on the fresh insight if it is suitable.

This process doesn't take much time (again, you are craving instant gratification) and makes it easier for you to resist giving in to temptation. The real trick is to change the physical feeling with the heart to bring about a shift in thoughts and eventually, actions. You don't suffocate or undermine your emotions.

Rather, you acknowledge them and then gently change them. When your emotions are slowly changing, the brain tows its line which makes us think in a way that lets us act according to our values and not on impulse or uncontrollable emotions.

Self-mastery is the master key
According to Walter Mischel, "Goal-directed and self-imposed gratification delay is fundamental to the process of emotional self-regulation." Emotional management, or regulation and the ability to control one's impulses, are vital to the concept of emotional intelligence.

Mischel's research established that while some people are born with a greater control for impulses, or better emotional management, others are not. A majority of people are somewhere in between. However, the good news is that emotional management, unlike intelligence, can be learned through practice. EQ isn't as genetically determined as cognitive abilities.

Impulse control and delayed gratification

Have you ever said something in anger and then regretted it immediately? Have you ever acted on an impulse or in haste only to regret it soon after the act? I can't even count the number of people who have lost their jobs, ruined their relationships, nixed their business negotiations, and blown away friendships because of that one moment when they acted on impulse. When you don't allow thoughts to take over and control your words or actions, you demonstrate low emotional intelligence.

Thus, the concept of emotional intelligence is closely connected with delaying gratification. We've all acted at some point or another without worrying about the consequences of our actions. Impulse control, or the ability to construct our thoughts and actions prior to speaking or acting, is a huge part of emotional control. You can manage your emotions more efficiently when you learn to override impulses, which is why impulse control is a huge part of emotional intelligence.

Ever wondered about the reason behind counting to ten, 100, or 1000 before reacting each time you are angry? We've all had our parents and educators counsel us about how anger can be restrained by counting up to ten or 100. It is simple, while you are in the process of counting, your emotional level is slowly decreasing. Once you are done with counting, the overpowering impulse to react to the emotion has passed. This allows you act in a more rational and thoughtful manner.

Emotional intelligence is about identifying these impulsive reactions and regulating them in a more positive and constructive manner. Rather than reacting mindlessly to a situation, you need to stop and think before responding. You choose to respond carefully instead of reacting impulsively to accomplish a more positive outcome or thwart a potentially uncomfortable situation.

Here are some useful tips for delaying gratification and boosting your ability to regulate emotions:

- **Have a clear vision for your future**
  Delaying gratification and controlling impulses or emotions becomes easier when you have a clear picture of the future. When you know what you want to accomplish five, eight, ten, or 15 years from now, it will be a lot easier to keep the bigger picture in mind if you come across temptations that can ruin your goal. Your 'why' (compelling reason for accomplishing a goal) will keep you sustained throughout the process of meeting the goal. Have a plan to fulfill your goal once you have a clear goal in mind. Identifying your goals and planning how you'll get there will help you resist the temptation more effectively.

- **Find ways to distract yourself from temptations and eliminate triggers**

For instance, if you are planning to quit drinking, take a different route back home from work if there are several bars along the way. Instead of focusing on what you can't do, concentrate on the activities you are passionate about. Surround yourself with positive people and activities that will help you dwell on your goal. Avoid trying to fill your time with material goods.

- **Make spending money difficult**

If you are a slave to plastic money and online transactions, you are making the process of spending money too easy for your own good. Paying with cold, hard cash can make you think several times before spending. You'll reconsider your purchases when you pay with real money rather than plastic. Take a part of your salary and put it into a separate account that you won't touch. Make sure that accessing your savings account won't be easy.

- **Avoid 'all or nothing' thinking**

Most of us think resisting temptation or giving up a bad habit is an 'all or nothing challenge.' It is natural for a majority of normal human beings to have a minor slip here and there. However, that doesn't mean you should just fall off and quit. Occasional slip-ups shouldn't be used as an excuse to get off the track. Despite a small detour, you can get back on the track. Don't try to convince yourself to wander in the opposite direction.

- **Make a list of common rationalizations**

Find a counterpoint or counterargument for each. For example, you were angry for just five minutes, or you are spending only ten dollars extra. Tell yourself that five minutes of anger is 150 minutes a month wasted in anger or ten dollars extra is $3,000 extra spent throughout the year.

Chapter 4: Boost Your Social EQ with These Powerful Verbal and Non-Verbal Clues

We've established in earlier chapters how emotional intelligence is the master key to effective leadership and social skills. By tuning into other people's emotions or by empathizing with how they feel, there is a higher chance that you will respond appropriately to create the desired positive result. Thus, our ability to connect with our own and other people's emotions can be a powerful tool in social and leadership situations.

Understanding other people, helping overcome stress situations, motivating your team, negotiating business deals, and building a close-knit social circle becomes easier when you can use the emotional information you have about them as leverage. It increases situational awareness and our ability to read people, thus helping us make the most positive decision.

Here are some verbal and non-verbal factors impacting social-emotional quotient, or our ability to read and deal with people:

Body language
Research reveals that body language accounts for 50 percent of our communication. You'd wonder why there were words in the first place if body

language accounts for half the communication process. Tuning in to a person's body language will help you pick up important signals related to their emotional state and subconscious thoughts or feelings.

Here's a quick cue sheet to reading people's feelings through their body language:

- Crossed arms and legs are signals of people creating a subconscious barrier. They are emotionally closed, suspicious, or do not subscribe to your ideas. They aren't open to listening to your views or are disinterested in the topic of conversation. You may have to emotionally open the person up a bit by changing the topic and then get back to the original topic. The physical act of uncrossing their arms and legs will make them more subconsciously receptive to your ideas.

- How can you tell a genuine smile from a fake one? Simple, it's all in the eyes. Observe that there's crinkled skin near the person's eyes forming crow's feet. People often present a happy expression to hide their true feelings. However, if their smile doesn't cause the skin around their eyes and mouth to crinkle, they are most likely not as happy as they are pretending to be.

Artificial smiles create wrinkles only around the mouth, while genuine smiles create wrinkles around the sides of the eyes.

- When people constantly take their gaze away from you while speaking, they are most likely not being very honest or trying to hide something. Similarly, if a person speaks to you without taking their gaze away from you for long, they may be trying to threaten or intimidate you with their gaze. It is alright to look away periodically. However, shifting gaze constantly is a red flag.

- When you are addressing a group of people, closely observe the ones who are nodding excessively or in a more exaggerated manner. These are the people who are most concerned about your approval. They are anxious about making a positive impression and want to be in your 'good books.'

- People who are nervous or anxious tend to fidget with their hands or objects. Other signs of nervousness also include excessive blinking, tapping feet, and constantly running one's hand over the face.

- When an entire group walks into the room, how do you analyze who the leader or decision maker is? Quickly observe everyone's posture. The leader will most likely walk with a straight posture, with shoulders pulled out. Subconsciously, they are trying to occupy maximum space to convey authority over their team. Standing straight and pulling back shoulders increases a person's physical frame. It makes them come across as much bigger than they actually are. This is why people in power love to keep this posture to show their influence over a group or place.

- Expressions are the windows into a person's emotional state. When a person is amazed or surprised, their eyebrows are raised, and the upper eyelids widen. Similarly, the mouth gapes open. Expressions can often overlap, so watch for micro expressions that can reveal precise emotions.

- For instance, raised eyebrows can also reveal fear. Look for other micro expression clues to determine the exact emotion. If a person is experiencing fear, the eyebrows will be raised and pulled together with tensed lower eyelids, while the two corners of their lips will appear stretched. Similarly, a person's surprise is expressed by eyebrows pulled up and a lowered jaw. Learn to read the entire face, especially micro expressions, if you want to learn more about how a person is feeling.

- Since micro expressions occur in fractions of seconds, they are virtually impossible to fake. For instance, notice how when people are being deceptive, their mouths will slightly angle differently. Similarly, their eye movements become more rapid, the nostrils flare a little bit, and they purse their lips together (a subconscious gesture signaling their lips are sealed, or they won't reveal the truth). Since these split expressions are driven by the subconscious, this makes them involuntary, and it is almost impossible to manipulate them.

- Enlarged pupils reveal intense emotions such as excitement, elation, delight, surprise, and interest. When a person is attracted to you or truly delighted to see you, their pupils will involuntarily enlarge.

- The direction of a person's feet can also determine what's going on in their mind. Since feet aren't the first thing on anyone's mind, it's harder to manipulate body language related to legs and feet. If a person's feet are pointing away from you, they are subconsciously signaling their need to escape. However, if their feet are pointed towards you, they are interested or in agreement with what you are saying.

- Typical signs of frustration and stress are clenched jaws, wrinkled eyebrows, and tensed neck. The person's words notwithstanding, if you observe any of these signs, he or she may be undergoing a stressful situation that they are trying to conceal. The trick for reading people's emotions accurately is to keep an eye out for a clear mismatch between verbal and non-verbal clues.

- Observe a person's walk to tune in to their feelings. People with a heavier gait along with low gravity while moving their legs are most likely hurt, stressed, frustrated, or depressed. People who walk with a slower and more relaxed pace are reflecting upon something. Notice how confident, happy, and goal-oriented people walk swiftly in one direction.

- Observing a person's eye movements is a near accurate way of gauging how he or she is feeling since our eye movements are connected to precise brain functions. Our eye movements have an established pattern depending on the brain function or type of information we are trying to access. For example, when a person is caught in an internal conflict or dilemma (to speak the truth or lie), they are more likely to look in the direction of their left collarbone. Darting sideways from one side to another can be a red flag that indicates deception.

- Proxemics is a subtopic within body language that talks about how people reveal their feelings and emotions through the physical distance they maintain with other people during the process of face-to-face interaction or communication. It is a very useful non-verbal signal for understanding a person's thought process or state of mind.

Psychologists and body language experts believe that the amount of physical distance we maintain while interacting with a person helps establish the dynamics of our relationship with them or reveals our emotions about them.

A person who isn't standing very close to you may not be emotionally open or receptive to you. They may have a tendency to closely guard their emotions or give only a little of themselves to the interaction. Such people may be more emotionally guarded and closed. You may need to make extra effort to get them to drop their guard and feel less intimidated. It may be a defense mechanism against being emotionally hurt or vulnerable.

On the other hand, if a person is leaning in your direction, they may subconsciously convey being emotionally open, or they trust you with their feelings. They may also be more interested in what you are speaking about.

Tone
The tone, volume, pitch, and emphasis of a person's voice can help you decode the hints that can help you tell what they are feeling. For example, if you notice plenty of inconsistencies in the tone of their voice as they speak, they are probably very angry, hurt, excited, or nervous. Ever notice how your voice shakes when you speak in a rage or are nervous about something? It can also be a sign the person is lying.

Similarly, if a person is speaking louder or softer than their regular volume, something may be amiss. Again, a person's tone is a dead giveaway. Sometimes people say something that sounds like a compliment. However, upon examining their tone closely, you realize the sarcasm and the condescension with which it was uttered.

The tone in which an individual ends their sentence says a lot about what they are trying to convey even with similar verbal clues. For example, if a person completes their sentence on a raised note, they are doubtful of something or are asking a question. Similarly, if they finish the sentence with a flat tone, they are pronouncing a statement or judgment. Watch out for how people end their sentences to get a clue about their inner feelings.

Again, the words people emphasize can help you uncover their true feelings. For example, if a person says, "Have you borrowed the blazer?" while emphasizing 'borrowed,' it indicates their doubt over whether you have borrowed, stolen, or done something else to the blazer. However, if the emphasis is on 'you,' they aren't sure if it is you or someone else who has borrowed the blazer.

I also like to look at pauses between phrases to know about the person's attitude, emotions, and intentions. For example, if a person pauses after saying something, it could be because what they just said is extremely important to them, or they truly believe in it. Sometimes, a person pauses to seek validation or feedback from others. The speaker wants to gauge your reaction to what they said since it is important for them.

When people are in a more emotionally unstable or negative frame of mind (angry, hurt, or upset), their voice tends to be higher pitched or squeaky. They are most likely losing a grip on their emotions or aren't able to regulate their emotions effectively. Notice how, when people are very angry, their voice becomes more screechy and squeaky, as if they are about to cry.

The speed of a speech
A person's emotions clearly impact the speed of their speech. Notice how you start talking much faster than your normal rate of speech, or words per minute, when you are angry or upset. A rapid speech can convey lack of organization, uncertainty, or lack of clarity. The person is not very comfortable with speaking and is just trying to finish throwing his or her words. Again, a slower than usual pace translates into low self-confidence, inability to express emotions, inability to come to terms with one's emotions, lack of emotional reassurance, and other similar feelings.

Verbal clues
A person's choice of words can say a lot about what they are thinking and feeling. Words are symbolic of our thoughts and feelings which, when combined with non-verbal clues, give us a comprehensive understanding of their emotional state.

The human brain is a miracle, really. When we think, or process rational and logical thoughts, we tend to use nouns and verbs. Conversely, when we attempt to express our thoughts or feelings in a verbal or written format, there is a tendency to use more adverbs and adjectives.

Any basic sentence features a subject and a verb. For example, "I walked." When a person adds more words to it, they can indicate their feelings or personality. For example, "I walked fast," can indicate a sense of urgency, fear, or insecurity. There are clear reasons why people use specific words over others.

Similarly, there is a hidden meaning behind what people say. Through their choice of words, people reveal emotions left unsaid.

Let's say you booked a table to take your family out for dinner at one of the fanciest, fine dining restaurants that recently opened in your neighborhood. The server greets you courteously and directs you to your table. What follows is an amazing dining experience.

The waiter introduces each of the seven courses in an informative yet engaging style, while you dine and enjoy wine in an upscale ambiance. After you enjoy a hearty meal and call for the tab, the waiter inquires if you enjoyed the food. You reply with, "The entrées were good."

The waiter doesn't look very delighted, even if what you said is a compliment in your opinion. Those four words you uttered reveal your real opinion about the food. It implies that other than the entrées, everything else was pretty average or the only thing that stood out during the entire meal were the entrées.

Did you actually say everything else other than the entrées was average? No. Then why did the waiter look crestfallen at your statement? It is obvious, people convey a lot not only through what they say but also through what they leave unsaid. Gather the hidden meaning or subtext behind what people say to tune in to their inner feelings. Notice how sometimes people will say, "You look very lovely today." It can either mean you look plain every day (which is a more passive-aggressive kind of statement), or you are looking exceptionally good today compared to other days.

Another powerful clue about what people are thinking or feeling is noticing how they talk about other people. In a research published in the *Journal of Personality and Social Psychology,* headed by Peter Harms and Simine Vazire of the University of Nebraska and University of St. Louis respectively, it was discovered that merely asking participants to rate positive and negative traits of three other people revealed a lot about the participants' social competence, general well-being, other people's perception of them, and their mental health.

It was observed that an individual's inclination to view other people in a positive manner was a strong indication of their own positive emotions. There is a strong link between seeing others in a more positive light and being emotionally stable, happy, productive, and enthusiastic.

On the other hand, viewing others in a negative light bears a strong correlation with a general sense of dissatisfaction, low self-esteem, anti-social behavior, and narcissism. People who hold plenty of negative emotions tend to perceive other people in a poorer or more negative light. This can also be an indication of emotional issues, mental health conditions, or a personality disorder. Again, emotions aren't good or bad but are reflections of how you are feeling. If a person experiences more negative emotions for others around them, it can be a clue to how they really feel about themselves.

If a person says that they 'made up their mind' after plenty of deliberation, the phrase indicates a mindset that is high on logic and rational thinking. The individual may be more contemplative and practical by nature. He or she may consider all the available options before making a decision. These are not your likely contenders for a snap of the moment decisions.

Do you know what metalanguage is? It is the intended words behind the words you speak. You don't say something directly but reveal it through the words you use. For example, notice how when people want to get someone to agree with what they've said, they'll always place yes, done, or okay followed by a question mark at the end. For example, "I can't hand in the project today. I'll submit it tomorrow, okay?" It is like manipulating the other person to agree.

To further increase your social-emotional quotient, pay attention to the sounds people utter, other than coherent words. Moaning, grunting, sighing, etc. can reveal a lot. Sometimes, these sounds will complement the words the speaker is using to make the message even more persuasive. However, at other times, there may be a mismatch between the person's words and sounds.

For example, someone may say, "I am having a really good day," followed by a sigh, which can indicate they are simply being sarcastic and are in fact having a bad day. You can even understand more about what a person really means when you observe their words and other miscellaneous sounds they make.

Environmental clues

A person's immediate environment says a lot about their emotional state. For instance, a messy, unclean, or disorganized space can indicate a lack of clarity of emotions or thoughts. Of course, everything has to be analyzed within a context. Someone may have an unkempt house because he or she is too busy to tidy it up and doesn't have housekeeping help.

All of us have certain spaces around us that are inaccessible that we don't really bother cleaning or organizing (space behind the cupboard or under the bed). These are spaces that we wouldn't normally clean. If such spaces are immaculately clean or organized, it can indicate anxiety or a disorder (obsessive-compulsive disorder).

Well-organized and clean spaces can indicate clarity of emotions or control over one's emotions. The person tends to be more reflective and introverted by nature. Similarly, people who are outwardly focused, or extroverts, tend to be surrounded by chaos.

This isn't pop psychology, but it is based on clear principles of how the environment around us is created through our actions, which themselves are directed by our subconscious thoughts and emotions. For example, using bright, vibrant, and bold prints in your décor or attire can be a sign of confidence, emotional self-assurance, and independence of thought or opinion. Likewise, a home with brighter and more vibrant colors is an indication of being bold, emotionally expressive, and outgoing. These people are not afraid of taking risks and are more than capable of understanding the needs and feelings of other people. More subtle colors imply inward directed emotions, or an introverted personality. These people may not be too receptive to another person's feelings and emotions.

People who hold on to old objects or hoard various objects can be excessively emotional, sensitive, or sentimental. They find it tough to move away from their past emotions or are still ridden by feelings of shame, regret, and guilt related to the past. These are people who latch on to old memories and can't release the emotions that hold them back.

When you use these verbal and non-verbal principles to understand people, your social-emotional quotient invariably increases.

Chapter 5: Secrets for Developing High Social E.I.

While our society is predictably emphasizing intelligence that is more tangible and visible (good grades), the one that goes largely overlooked and ignored is our ability to conduct ourselves in social situations. The knack of regulating our emotions in social settings in addition to being able to understand other people's feelings is our master key to success. While everyone is working hard on their book smarts, social smarts are also vital and, in fact, are proven to be more important than intelligence quotient.

Take for instance, a scenario where you are interviewing two candidates for a leadership role. Joanne is slightly more qualified, skilled, and experienced than Rose. However, Rose has the ability to understand people, works as a team player, and she can also inspire and motivate a team to accomplish higher targets. Joanne is high on technical skills but not very effective in understanding and managing people's emotions.

Who will you hire as a recruitment manager?

Obviously, Rose. The ability to understand and channel people's emotions in the best way possible is a priceless tool in today's world.

Social Intelligence (SI) is our ability to build relationships and figure out our way through social environments.

Here are some lesser known secrets that can increase your social-emotional intelligence by several fold:

Adopt and adapt
Don't fight your instinct to mirror another person's condition all the time. Human beings are wired to mirror the feelings and emotions of those around us. This is empathy! We naturally feel what others are feeling. However, at times we often take the high road and try to fight this feeling of mirroring the other person's emotions. For example, say your spouse is upset and screaming at you. You know they are angry.

However, you've read how important it is to pacify the situation by not reacting in a similar manner. You choose to stay calm. Then, you try to calm down your partner. This is where more trouble begins. The angry partner feels 'you don't understand them,' 'you don't understand what they are trying to say,' or 'you never get them.' In your view, you were simply trying to pacify the potentially volatile situation. How did it backfire?

This happens when, sometimes, instead of adapting to the emotions of the other person, we try to take the high road to fight mirroring their feelings. Rather, put yourself where your partner is and adopt his or her emotional state of mind. This may help you gain a good perspective of how they are feeling. It also helps them know that you understand where they are coming from, which makes the situation less unfriendly.

Practice being assertive, not aggressive
One of the secrets of being socially intelligent is learning to be more assertive without being aggressive. Assertive people know how not to please people all the time without offending them.

Assertiveness is a reasonable and genuine statement of opinions and feelings. "I would really prefer going to the games this weekend." This is an assertive statement.

You are making your needs clear without being aggressive or demanding. Aggressiveness is marked by a clear lack of respect for the needs and rights of other people. When you are aggressive, you are looking at things only from a selfish perspective or seeking to satisfy a self-filling goal. The aggressive version of the above statement would be, "We're good for the games this weekend."

You are pronouncing your statement more as a judgment without respect or concern for the other person.

On the other hand, assertiveness is characterized by respect and understanding for the other person's feelings or opinion, even though you may not agree with it. While aggressive says, "Only I am right," assertive says, "Though your opinion doesn't agree with mine, I respect it. We can agree to disagree."

Assertive people don't let others take advantage of them and know where to draw the line without being harsh. They know when to say 'no' to people without hurting their feelings. When you demonstrate respect for a person or group of people, the hurt is reduced. Assertive is making your stand clear while showing respect.

However, when you display lack of respect or concern for the other person's feelings, opinion, or desires, you are treading on aggression. Assertive people are unafraid of standing up for their values. They don't shy away from expressing their needs and goals to others. Assertive folks treat others as equals and operate from the point of mutual respect. They don't intend to hurt people and themselves. These are the people who are always seeking a win-win situation.

Aggressive people have a deep desire to win and operate from a point of disrespecting or overlooking other people's needs. They see hurting or disrespecting others as a by-product of winning or being successful. Aggressive folks are more focused on proving themselves right rather than arriving at a win-win solution. They have mastered the art of feeding on other people's insecurities and fears.

Social and emotional intelligence is about being assertive and respecting other people's needs and opinion while spelling out your own needs and opinion. As a leader, one must be assertive to make themselves clear while still showing respect and empathy towards the team. Even if you don't agree with someone, you must attempt to understand where they are coming from to boost your social-emotional quotient along with your social skills.

Here are some tips for boosting your assertiveness:

- **Keep communication genuine and open**
  Actively listen to the other person's opinions, needs, feelings, and desires. Watch out for verbal and non-verbal signals to understand them more effectively. Don't listen to respond or react, listen to understand. Similarly, listen without interrupting the other person. Let them finish what they say before you dive in with your take!

- **Don't be guilty**
  Don't feel guilty about refusing someone if it doesn't fit with your scheme of things. At the same time, listen to people without making them feel guilty for communicating their needs.

- **Stay calm and balanced**

Even in a tense or potentially volatile situation, maintain eye contact, keep a relaxed expression, and speak in a steady, even tone. Assertive people seldom let their emotions control their actions. They have a good grip on themselves and can maintain composure even in the most stressful situations.

- **Practice assertiveness before a mirror**

Pretend you are talking to a friend who is urging you to do something you don't want to do. How will you convey it to them in an open and honest manner? Focus on your words, body language, expressions, voice, and tone.

- **Always see people as allies and not enemies**

In the workplace setting, think collaboration and not competition.

- **Stick with 'I' statements**

For instance, instead of saying, "We should not go there," try saying, "I don't think we should go there." It makes you come across as firm without being pushy. You are expressing your thoughts without issuing a summons, which reveals respect for the other person.

- **Stay patient**
  If you are not an assertive person, it won't come overnight. Commit to being more mindful of your verbal and non-verbal communication while speaking to people for demonstrating greater assertiveness.

- **Respect differences in opinion**
  Realize that just because someone doesn't hold the same opinion as you, that doesn't mean he or she is wrong or bad. Agree to disagree and empathize with people even if you don't agree with them. Try to understand where they are coming from and what drives them to think the way they do.

Try to keep a win-win, problem-solution approach rather than proving your point or being obsessed with winning. During situations where you're in conflict with another person, avoid viewing the other person as an enemy. Rather, focus on a win-win solution that resolves the situation for everyone involved.

Practice empathy

Empathy is the ability to put yourself in someone else's shoes and feel their feelings or emotions exactly as they experience it. It is the ability to understand and experience other people's emotions as if it were happening to you. Predictably, the ability to experience other people's emotions and to leverage this experience for helping someone feel better about the situation is a much sought-after skill in today's world.

Empathy is the cornerstone of social-emotional intelligence. By empathizing with people, you can reach out to them and manage their emotions more efficiently. The ability to know how someone is feeling can be used to motivate, inspire, lead, and influence people in a positive manner.

Here are the top secrets for developing greater empathy:

- Traveling periodically to experience different places, cultures, lifestyles, and beliefs is a great way to develop empathy and appreciation for people whose lives are different from yours. You'll develop a better understanding and appreciation of people who are different from you. There will be a keener understanding of why they think and act the way they do.

- Examine your covert and overt biases. Most of us operate with certain biases centered on race, gender, age, education, profession, etc. They act as an obstacle when it comes to empathizing or listening to people. Make a list of biases that you think you possess and try to read opinions that are contrary to your biases. Look for evidence that challenges your thinking and gradually try to overcome these biases.

- Nurture a productive curiosity. You can learn something from an 'inexperienced subordinate,' a 'picky client,' or a 'hotheaded boss.' Rather than labeling people, develop a sense of curiosity about what you can genuinely learn from them. This will lead to a stronger understanding and appreciation of the people around you.

- Volunteer at an NGO or charity organization in your free time. It will not only help you appreciate what you already have but will also facilitate greater empathy for people who aren't as fortunate as you. The knowledge that you made a positive impact on someone's life will make you feel better about yourself. When you spend time with the less fortunate, you develop the ability to understand other people's challenges and problems, which in turn boosts your empathy factor.

- During situations where there is a conflict because of a difference in opinion, a resolution becomes easier when you understand the other party's underlying fears, needs, and motivations. Even when they are negative towards you, you'll understand why. Watch debates (especially during elections) to appreciate different points of view and understand why people think the way they do. If you find yourself tilting in any one direction, quickly look for evidence that is contrary to your stand. This will help you develop the ability to appreciate multiple points of view without being dogmatic about your stand. At its essence, empathy is about developing a greater understanding of another person's point of view or situation even when you don't necessarily agree with them.

- Practice predicting how a person will act or react in a certain situation by placing yourself in their shoes. This will give you greater insight and perceptiveness into how people feel about any given situation.

- Be fully present by keeping away your phone, turning off your email alerts, and mindfully listening to the other person. According to the research conducted by a professor at UCLA, things we speak make up for only seven percent of the message we are trying to communicate.

The other 93 percent is determined by our body language and tone of voice. You are missing important clues if you aren't fully focusing on the other person while communicating with them.

They may be saying something that is contrary to what they feel, which you will miss if you are too preoccupied to focus on their non-verbal signals.

- Smiles are infectious. It rarely happens that someone smiles at you, and you don't smile in return. It the fastest way to connect with people and show solidarity or empathy towards them. A simple smile can boost feel-good hormones within the brain and stimulate its reward centers. You'll do yourself and others a whole lot of good by smiling.

- Address people by their names and praise them publicly. What is it that you heard about praising people publicly and admonishing them in private? Efficient leaders have mastered the art of using people's names while addressing them and using more encouraging statements. Make each person feel important by highlighting their skills or accomplishments in public. This inspires them to do even better work. Even when a person's performance slips, keep referring to accomplishments in public to remind them of their true potential. People respond wonderfully to praise.

- Give specific compliments to people. Your empathy and social-emotional quotient will increase when you learn to be more specific while appreciating people. For example, instead of saying, "You did a good job," tell someone, "The project was very well-researched and thorough despite the fact that the topic was complex and extensive," or, "Would you like to share the inspiration behind your brilliant sales growth concept?"

Be a listening champ

We saw how listening is intrinsic to the process of assertiveness and empathy, both of which are vital for boosting your social-emotional quotient.

Listening isn't only about hearing out what people are saying. It is also figuring out what they leave unspoken through their body language, voice, emotions, and choice of words. Let us consider an example to better understand how listening (or tuning in to verbal and non-verbal patterns) is integral to the process of communication.

It's Friday evening, and after a hectic week at work, everyone is getting ready to let their hair down over the weekend. They are shutting down their computers and getting ready to leave when the company CEO, Sue, walks in and informs them that the deadline for the project they've been working so hard on is pushed ahead by two weeks.

Everyone is naturally disappointed and stressed. The project head sits silently at her desk wondering how to comply with the deadline. The project manager, Ann, says, "We will still do a good job and submit the project according to the new deadline." Another employee, Dan, gets to work on his computer, and few people leave the office. A majority of team members say they can handle the new adjustments. Sue leaves the office thinking like it went way better than she thought it would.

What she didn't catch was the inconsistency in the body language and words of the project manager, who left the office in a rage, while she replied to an email from a prospective recruiter. Other team members went to grab a coffee and were almost in tears from the newfound stress they will face.

Yes, no one told Sue how they truly felt when she asked for feedback. So, how was she supposed to know how they really felt about the deadline being pushed? Do you think she was in any way responsible for not understanding her employees' feelings? Of course, she didn't really listen or tune in to what they were trying to convey. She went by their words but failed to catch what they left unsaid. A major part of social-emotional intelligence is to understand what people leave unsaid.

Here are some tips to develop ace listening skills:

- Keep an open mind. Avoid operating with a pre-conditioned, or prejudiced, mind and be more open to listening to people without labeling or criticizing them. I'd say one of the biggest challenges in the process of communication is listening to people without jumping to conclusions. Don't attempt to hijack the conversation or try to finish their sentences. Remember, the person is communicating their ideas, thoughts, opinions, and feelings. Let them freely express themselves without being interrupted.

- We often spend more time planning what we are going to say in response to something rather than actively listening to a person to understand them. Don't listen to respond. Listen to understand what the person is trying to convey. Focus completely on what the speaker is saying rather than rehearsing your responses. Even if something seems uninteresting, listen to it.

- Wait for the speaker to pause before asking questions or clarifying doubts. Don't interrupt someone in the middle of their speech. Rather, hold your questions until they pause. "Let us go back a few seconds. I didn't really understand what you meant by XYZ." Sometimes our questions can throw people in a totally different direction from where they intend to take the conversation. When the speaker is going in a different direction, get them back on the original topic by saying something like, "It was wonderful knowing about ABC, but tell us more about XYZ now."

Conclusion

Thank you for making it through to the end of this book, let's hope it was informative and was able to provide you with all the tools you need to achieve your goals.

I hope you enjoyed reading it and that you were able to learn the finer aspects of emotional intelligence, self-awareness, and social relationships. I also hope it offered you plenty of inspiring ideas, practical tips, and nuggets of wisdom about boosting your emotional quotient, or emotional intelligence.

The best part is, unlike intelligence quotient, emotional quotient can be developed through regular practice, training, and application. Improving your emotional intelligence is a continuous and dynamic process that helps you enhance your skills over time.

The next step is to simply go out there and use all the proven strategies mentioned in the book. You can't become more emotionally intelligent overnight by reading about it. Apply the techniques mentioned in the book in your everyday life to witness results!

You'll gradually transform from an emotionally incompetent individual who struggles with their own and other people's emotions to an emotionally evolved and socially adept individual, who will enjoy better interpersonal relationships and professional success in life.

www.ingramcontent.com/pod-product-compliance
Lightning Source LLC
Chambersburg PA
CBHW071951070526
44583CB00015B/1151